EXCEL FORMULAS NINJA

HENRY E. MEJIA

EXCEL FORMULAS NINJA

Copyright © 2020 HENRY E. MEJIA

DEDICATION

To my parents, who have taught me that life is about overcoming obstacles and enjoying it.

CONTENTS

ACKNOWLEDGMENTS

I would like to thank all those who supported me throughout the creation of this book, either with words of encouragement or with ideas to improve it.

INTRODUCTION

Welcome to a new EXCEL NINJA book! The fastest, the most practice-based and definitely the most straightforward Excel Book Series you will ever find!

You will learn to use with confidence the most important and useful Excel Formulas.

Excel Ninja Series is all about this:

- **Learning fast**
- **Having fun while learning**
- **Learning trough practice (from the very beginning)**
- **No unnecessary fillers to make the book look longer**

- **The most straightforward and lean approach**
- **Getting results!**

Loaded with a gigantic amount of practice spreadsheets, examples, and recommendations.

My goal for this Excel Ninja Series was to achieve the perfect balance between a lot of exercises and examples without compromising the straightforward approach, and that's what you will find here!

That being said, I would like to summarize the benefits of becoming an Excel FORMULAS Ninja:

- Increased chances of getting a promotion and better jobs (Because you are more productive and have better skills)
- Less workload (Excel does the heavy lifting)
- More free time
- Less stress

- A sense of growth (When you learn something new you feel great, and you know it!)
- Etc., etc.

I could spend more time, word and pages explaining to you the benefits and the importance of becoming an EXCEL FORMULAS NINJA, but I promised that I won't fill this book with unnecessary words so let's start the first chapter right now!

GET YOUR 40 PRACTICE SPREADSHEETS (.XLSX)

Before starting Chapter 1 I recommend you to get your 40 practice spreadsheets. Those exercise files are included for everyone who purchases this book. They will serve you at the end of each chapter to reinforce what you have learned and make sure you have learned it well.

All you have to do is to send me an email to:

ems.online.empire@gmail.com

With the Subject *"FORMULAS NINJA PRACTICE SPREADSHEETS"* and saying:

"Hello, I bought your book EXCEL FORMULAS NINJA and I need the 40

practice spreadsheets"

I will gladly reply your email and send you the files.

Now you are ready to start Chapter 1. Let's go!

CHAPTER 1:

BASIC THINGS ABOUT FUNCTIONS

WHAT IS A FUNCTION?

A Function is a formula that you can use in Microsoft Excel in order to get an automatic result based on the values that you entered in that formula. So, from now on, Functions and Formulas are the same, ok?

There are lots of different functions that perform different calculations (too many of them) so learning them all is almost impossible and not time effective because you won't use them all. So, my advice to you is the next one:

1. Learn the most useful functions first

2. Figure out which other function you need to learn in order to complete your work

3. You will find that, in most situations, the formula you need is explained in this book.

Through Excel Functions Ninja you will learn the most useful and important functions for your work and life!

HOW CAN YOU USE FUNCTIONS IN EXCEL?

When you open an Excel spreadsheet, you will find the "Formulas" section, and then you have 2 options:

- **Option A:** Click the "Insert Function" icon and choose the function

- **Option B:** Click in the "Category" you want (Recently used, Financial, Logical, Text) and then choose the Function.

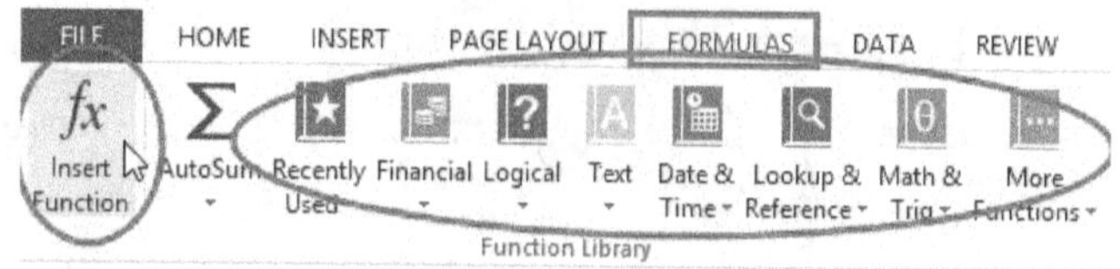

However, I don't like neither of those options because it takes too much time. **It is easier to simply click on the cell where you want to write the formula and write**

=NAMEOFTHEFUNCTION(

WHAT IS THAT? Well, every formula has its own name, that way Excel identifies what you want to do.

- Writing **=** is the way you say to Excel that you are starting a function or formula
- The different **NamesOfTheFunctions** is what you are going to learn

- Writing **(** means that you will start to add values to the formula, so it can calculate what you want

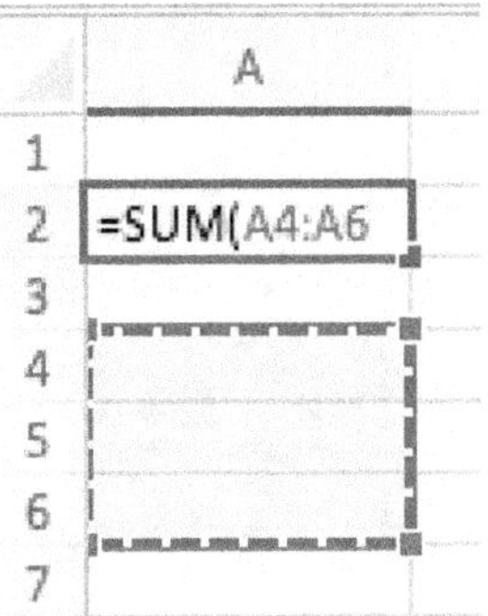

Here you can see that the Name of the function is **SUM** and the values that I'm writing are **CELLS A4, A5 and A6. (A4:A6 is the whole range or matrix involving those 3 Cells)**

Another example here. The name of the

Function is **IF**, and I'm using different Cells to give an order to Excel.

That's the way we use functions.

HOW CAN I EDIT FUNCTIONS IN EXCEL?

You can do that by double clicking in the cell that has the function. That way you will be able to change the function or the values within the parenthesis.

HOW ARE FUNCTIONS STRUCTURED IN EXCEL?

Basically, any function is structured (divided) in parts, called Arguments, that are written inside the parenthesis.

=FUNCTION(Argument 1,Argument 2,Argument 3,......)

Some of the functions have just 1 argument, some of them more than one. Some of the functions have optional arguments and some of them just have mandatory arguments.

HOW ARE THE FUNCTIONS CATEGORIZED IN THIS EXCEL NINJA BOOK?

I decided to categorize them in groups that make sense and are easy to remember.

1. Arithmetic functions
2. Ranking and Statistics
3. Search
4. Financial
5. Conditional (Logical)
6. Text handling
7. Date
8. Combined functions (the exact name is "Nested functions")

That's it! Let's go to chapter 2!

QUICK CHAPTER SUMMARY

- Functions are sometimes called Formulas
- Each function has its own name
- Functions have parts that are called Arguments
- Functions in this book are divided into different categories so you can learn them easily

CHAPTER 2:

ARITHMETIC FUNCTIONS

This is where you begin your journey to becoming an Excel Functions Ninja! Let's Start with the Arithmetic functions.

IMPORTANT NOTE:

IN THIS CHAPTER YOU WILL ALSO LEARN SOME IMPORTANT DYNAMICS OF THE FUNCTIONS LIKE

- *DRAGGING FORMULAS*
  (duplicating the formulas to save time)

- ***ABSOLUTE REFERENCES*** *(fixing the cells so when you drag the formula, the cells within the formula aren't dragged too)*

SUM FUNCTION

WHAT IS THIS FUNCTION FOR?

Sum Function's main purpose is to ADD (to sum) all the values that you want. You do that by manually inserting the CELLS in to the formula.

WHICH IS THE MAIN BENEFIT OF THIS FORMULA?

You can use Excel as a calculator AND you can "drag" the formula to automatically perform more sums in another part of the spreadsheet.

In simple words, you can write one formula and perform 10, 20, or 100 calculations in no time!

HOW IS THIS FUNCTION STRUCTURED?

The syntax (Structure) of the SUM function is the next one:

$$=SUM(cell1,cell2,cell3,cell4,....)$$

Or

$$=SUM(Cell1:Cell20)$$

WHAT DOES THAT MEAN?

=SUM(cell1,cell2,cell3,cell4,....) means that you can insert to the formula the name of one cell (by example A1), the separate that by a comma **","** and insert another cell (by example A2).

$$=SUM(A1,A2)$$

This would mean that you want to sum the value in A1 plus the value in A2.

=SUM(Cell1:Cell20) means that you can also insert a "Range" (a matrix) to the formula to sum the whole bunch of values within that range.

The first part of the range needs to be the upper left cell, the separated by a double period ":" and the second part of the range is the bottom right cell.

$$=SUM(A1:C20)$$

This would mean that you want to sum ALL THE VALUES within that range. The values of that range are from A1 to A2, from B1 to B20 and from C1 to C20. (60 cells in total)

EXERCISE! (Open file Chapter2ex1.xlsx)

We will sum the numbers in the file, and the sum needs to appear in the cell B7

	A	B	C
1			
2	1256		
3			2749
4	1783		
5			9826
6			
7			

Step 1: Start writing the formula in Cell B7

=SUM

Step 2: Open the parenthesis

=SUM(

Step 3: Click the first cell (A2) and THEN add a comma

=SUM(A2,

IMPORTANT NOTE:

THIS STEP OF CLICKING IN THE CELL IS GOING TO BE USED DURING THE WHOLE BOOK TO INSERT THE CELLS TO THE FORMULA

Step 4: Click the second cell (A4) and THEN add another comma

$$=SUM(A2,A4,$$

Step 5: Repeat until you add all the cells, **CLOSE THE PARENTHESIS AND PRESS ENTER!**

$$=SUM(A2,A4,C3,C5)$$

	A	B	C
1			
2	1256		
3			2749
4	1783		
5			9826
6			
7		=SUM(A2,A4,C3,C5)	

Step 6: You get the result

$$15614$$

EXERCISE! (Open file Chapter2ex2.xlsx)

NOTE: By the way, during all this journey we will be practicing with examples that involve superheroes (maybe you will recognize some of them, maybe you won't) to make it just a little fun. Sometimes learning Excel could be tedious and boring but with this "superhero approach" it is possible that you have a better time!

These examples are meant to serve you equally well in this practice than in your real life at work! The formulas are the same and the application of those formulas are the same, we are just having a "theme-based training here".

Now you have a database about the income received by each super hero by day. You need to sum the range in order to get the total earnings (all of the heroes and all of the days). Doing that cell by cell is time-consuming, so we will use the range. By the way, they are super rich! They earn a lot of money!

Step 1: Start writing the formula in A1 (Remember the parenthesis, this is mandatory for EVERY function)

$$=SUM($$

Step 2: Select the whole range and **close the parenthesis, AND PRESS ENTER**

	A	B	C	D	E	F	G
1	=SUM(B2:G10	DAY 1	DAY 2	DAY 3	DAY 4	DAY 5	DAY 6
2	The Avengers	$3,188	$8,415	$8,826	$6,873	$4,326	$3,449
3	Doc Savage	$6,698	$7,072	$5,084	$2,297	$7,815	$7,147
4	Vegeta	$3,254	$1,209	$7,210	$6,251	$5,763	$5,824
5	Ron Weasley	$4,047	$9,351	$7,597	$3,659	$1,524	$8,207
6	The Shadow	$6,652	$2,270	$6,524	$9,477	$2,127	$3,879
7	Hellboy	$9,052	$3,834	$9,662	$7,127	$9,942	$2,566
8	Incredible Hulk	$9,962	$7,582	$2,844	$9,958	$7,508	$3,922
9	Rambo	$6,008	$9,063	$9,420	$6,954	$7,990	$3,642
10	Sarah Connor	$7,629	$5,616	$3,624	$8,090	$7,773	$2,142
11							

$$=SUM(B2:G10)$$

Step 3: Get the result!

	A
1	$ 327,925

EXERCISE (Open file Chapter2ex3.xlsx)

Now I'm interested in knowing how

much money was paid to them by each day so now you need to sum EACH COLUMN! How can you do that? Easy, just sum each column (as a range) and DRAG the formula for it to sum the other columns automatically.

Step 1: Start writing the formula in Cell B10

=SUM(

Step 2: Select the whole range and **close the parenthesis, AND PRESS ENTER**

	A	B	
1	Green Lantern	$ 3,188	$
2	Storm	$ 6,698	$
3	Vegeta	$ 3,254	$
4	Ron Weasley	$ 4,047	$
5	The Shadow	$ 6,652	$
6	Hellboy	$ 9,052	$
7	Incredible Hulk	$ 9,962	$
8	Rambo	$ 6,008	$
9	Sarah Connor	$ 7,629	$
10		=SUM(B1:B9	
11			

Step 3: TO DRAG A FORMULA,

CLICK IN TO THE CELL THAT HAS A FORMULA (IN THIS CASE B10), AND IN THE BOTTOM RIGN PART OF THE CELL YOU WILL SEE A CROSS. WHEN YOU SEE THE CROSS, CLICK, HOLD AND DRAG THE FORMULA TO WHERE YOU CWANT TO COPY IT.

	A	B	C	D	E	F	G
1		3188	8415	8826	6873	4326	3449
2		6698	7072	5084	2297	7815	7147
3		3254	1209	7210	6251	5763	5824
4		4047	9351	7597	3659	1524	8207
5		6652	2270	6524	9477	2127	3879
6		9052	3834	9662	7127	9942	2566
7		9962	7582	2844	9958	7508	3922
8		6008	9063	9420	6954	7990	3642
9		7629	5616	3624	8090	7773	2142
10		56490					
11							

Step 4: You will automatically cloned the formula and that each formula sums its column, that is because when you dragged the formula, you also dragged the cells within the formula

	A	B	C	D	
1	Green Lantern	$ 3,188	$ 8,415	$ 8,826	$
2	Storm	$ 6,698	$ 7,072	$ 5,084	$
3	Vegeta	$ 3,254	$ 1,209	$ 7,210	$
4	Ron Weasley	$ 4,047	$ 9,351	$ 7,597	$
5	The Shadow	$ 6,652	$ 2,270	$ 6,524	$
6	Hellboy	$ 9,052	$ 3,834	$ 9,662	$
7	Incredible Hulk	$ 9,962	$ 7,582	$ 2,844	$
8	Rambo	$ 6,008	$ 9,063	$ 9,420	$
9	Sarah Connor	$ 7,629	$ 5,616	$ 3,624	$
10		$ 56,490	$ 54,412	D1:D9)	$ 6
11					

The explanation of this function was longer because I needed to explain clearly **Ranges and Formula Dragging.** Those are basic concepts that we are going to use ALWAYS THROUGOUT this book, so you need to understand them well!

AVERAGE FUNCTION

WHAT IS THIS FUNCTION FOR?

Its main purpose is to average a set of values in many cells. It can handle up to 255 values to average per formula.

WHICH IS THE MAIN BENEFIT OF THIS FORMULA?

You can average quickly and clone the formula (dragging it) so have multiple averages.

HOW IS THIS FUNCTION STRUCTURED?

The syntax (Structure) of the **AVERAGE** function is the next one:

=AVERAGE(cell1,cell2,cell3,cell4,….)

Or

=AVERAGE(Cell1:Cell20)

WHAT DOES THAT MEAN?

It functions in similar way of the SUM function (the structure is very similar) but instead of adding, it will calculate the Average.

EXERCISE (Open file Chapter2ex4.xlsx)

Now you need to get the daily income average for each superhero!

Step 1: Start writing your first formula in B13 (we will drag the formula later)

=AVERAGE(B4:B12)

Why? Because we want the average from the range B4 to B12

Step 2: Press Enter to get the result. Then, drag the formula to get the averages for the other days!

	DAY 1	DAY 2	DAY 3
Robin	$ 3,188	$ 8,415	$ 8,826
Captain Marvel	$ 6,698	$ 7,072	$ 5,084

Picollo	$ 3,254	$ 1,209	$ 7,210
Batman	$ 4,047	$ 9,351	$ 7,597
The Rocketeer	$ 6,652	$ 2,270	$ 6,524
Superman	$ 9,052	$ 3,834	$ 9,662
Batwoman	$ 9,962	$ 7,582	$ 2,844
Hawkeye	$ 6,008	$ 9,063	$ 9,420
The Incredibles	$ 7,629	$ 5,616	$ 3,624
	$ 6,276.67	$ 6,045.78	$ 6,754.56

Congratulations! Now you know how to use AVERAGE!

MIN FUNCTION

WHAT IS THIS FUNCTION FOR?

Its main purpose is to find and return the lowest value within a set of cells (normally a range of cells)

WHICH IS THE MAIN BENEFIT OF THIS FORMULA?

You can get multiple lowest values and the same time.

HOW IS THIS FUNCTION STRUCTURED?

The syntax (Structure) of the **MIN** function is the next one:

$$=MIN(cell1,cell2,cell3,cell4,....)$$

Or

$$=MIN(Cell1:Cell20)$$

WHAT DOES THAT MEAN?

It functions in similar way of the AVERAGE function (the structure is very similar) but instead of getting the average, it will return the lowest value.

EXERCISE (Open file Chapter2ex5.xlsx)

You have the same superheroes and now you need to find the lowest income IN ONE DAY per each superhero.

Step 1: Write the first formula at H4 (Select the range required)

$$=MIN(B4:G4)$$

	A	B	C	D	E	F	G	H
3		DAY 1	DAY 2	DAY 3	DAY 4	DAY 5	DAY 6	LOWEST
4	Robin	$ 3,188	$ 8,415	$ 8,826	$ 6,873	$ 4,326	$ 3,449	=MIN(B4:G4
5	Captain Marvel	$ 6,698	$ 7,072	$ 5,084	$ 2,297	$ 7,815	$ 7,147	

(sorry about the image, but you can open the file in Excel)

Why? Because we want to find the lowest value PER EACH SUPERHERO. That is why you have a horizontal range.

Step 2: Press enter and drag the formula down.

LOWEST

Robin	$ 3,188
Captain Marvel	$ 2,297
Picollo	$ 1,209

Batman	$	1,524
The Rocketeer	$	2,127
Superman	$	2,566
Batwoman	$	2,844
Hawkeye	$	3,642
The Incredibles	$	2,142

Now you know how to use the MIN function! Congrats!

MAX FUNCTION

WHAT IS THIS FUNCTION FOR?

Its main purpose is to find and return the greatest value within a set of cells (normally a range of cells)

WHICH IS THE MAIN BENEFIT OF

THIS FORMULA?

You can get multiple greatest values and the same time.

HOW IS THIS FUNCTION STRUCTURED?

The syntax (Structure) of the **MAX** function is the next one:

=MAX(cell1,cell2,cell3,cell4,....)

Or

=MAX(Cell1:Cell20)

WHAT DOES THAT MEAN?

It is almost exactly the same as MIN function) but instead of getting the lowest value, it will return the greatest value.

EXERCISE (Open file Chapter2ex6.xlsx)

Now try to find the greatest income IN ONE DAY per each superhero.

Step 1: Write the first formula at I4 (Select the range required)

$$=MAX(B4:G4)$$

	A	B	C	D	E	F	G	H	I
3		DAY 1	DAY 2	DAY 3	DAY 4	DAY 5	DAY 6	LOWEST	GREATEST
4	Robin	$ 3,188	$ 8,415	$ 8,826	$ 6,873	$ 4,326	$ 3,449	$ 3,188	=MAX(B4:G4)

Why? Because we want to find the greatest value PER EACH SUPERHERO. That is why you have a horizontal range.

Step 2: Press enter and drag the formula down.

GREATEST

	GREATEST
Robin	$ 8,826
Captain Marvel	$ 7,815
Picollo	$ 7,210
Batman	$ 9,351

The Rocketeer	$	9,477
Superman	$	9,942
Batwoman	$	9,962
Hawkeye	$	9,420
The Incredibles	$	8,090

Great! This one was easy because you already knew the MIN function!

COUNT FUNCTION

WHAT IS THIS FUNCTION FOR?

Its main purpose is to count the number of cells that have some value written in them (and ignore the empty ones) within a range, and to return the total amount.

It counts cells with numbers and text at the same time.

WHICH IS THE MAIN BENEFIT OF THIS FORMULA?

It is used find the number of cells that have something written.

HOW IS THIS FUNCTION STRUCTURED?

The syntax (Structure) of the **COUNT** function is the next one:

=COUNT(cell1,cell2,cell3,cell4,….)

Or

=COUNT(Cell1:Cell20)

WHAT DOES THAT MEAN?

It is almost exactly the same as MIN, MAX and SUM functions. It will return the number of full cells within a range

EXERCISE (Open file Chapter2ex7.xlsx)

Here we have our heroes, working hard to save people (and to earn money to pay the bills). You need to figure out how many days did each hero work, and how many heroes worked each day. So you need to use the COUNT function in horizontal and vertical way.

Step 1: Start writing your formula in B13

=COUNT(

Step 2: Select the Range of cells. In this situation you will need the whole Monday column (to figure out how many heroes worked that day)

=COUNT(B4:B12)

Step 3: Drag the formula to the right!

Step 4: Repeat the process to find the work days but now by each hero. And drag the formula down.

=COUNT(B4:G4)

	MON	TUE	WED	THU	FRI	SAT	
Goku	$ 3,188		$ 8,826	$ 6,873		$ 3,449	4
Rocky Balboa	$ 6,698	$ 7,072	$ 5,084	$ 2,297	$ 7,815	$ 7,147	6
Obi Wan Kenobi		$ 1,209	$ 7,210		$ 5,763		3
Jack Sparrow	$ 4,047	$ 9,351		$ 3,659	$ 1,524	$ 8,207	5
Supergirl	$ 6,652	$ 2,270	$ 6,524		$ 2,127	$ 3,879	5
Han Solo	$ 9,052		$ 9,662	$ 7,127		$ 2,566	4
Wolverine		$ 7,582	$ 2,844	$ 9,958	$ 7,508	$ 3,922	5
Neo	$ 6,008	$ 9,063		$ 6,954			3
Thor	$ 7,629	$ 5,616	$ 3,624	$ 8,090	$ 7,773	$ 2,142	6
	7	7	7	7	6	7	

With this formula we found that Thor and Rocky were the most active heroes during the week, they worked 6 days! While Obi Wan Kenobi simply didn't want to work that much, what a shame!

At the same time, we found that Friday was the least active day of the week. I guess some heroes need a break.

That is how you use the COUNT Function!

SUBTOTAL FUNCTION

WHAT IS THIS FUNCTION FOR?

Its main purpose is to be a flexible function with which you can choose between different arithmetic operations (such as SUM, AVERAGE, MIN, MAX, COUNT) within the same function!

WHICH IS THE MAIN BENEFIT OF THIS FORMULA?

You can change the arithmetic operation you want to perform without having to write another function.

HOW IS THIS FUNCTION STRUCTURED?

The syntax (Structure) of the **SUBTOTAL** function is the next one:

=SUBTOTAL(Function number,cells)

WHAT DOES THAT MEAN?

Argument 1 Function number: You can choose between different arithmetic operations using the "Function Number" that corresponds to the one that you want.

The most used are the following:

NUMBER 1 FOR AVERAGE

NUMBER 2 FOR COUNT

NUMBER 4 FOR MAX

NUMBER 5 FOR MIN

NUMBER 9 FOR SUM

As you can notice, you know how to use those functions already, but with SUBTOTAL you can have all of them at once.

EXERCISE (Open file Chapter2ex8.xlsx)

Step 1: Start writing the formula in B13. Let's start trying with the average Income per day.

$$=SUBTOTAL(1,B4:B12)$$

Why? Because we want the Average (the number you need is 1) income for Monday.

Step 2: When you drag the formula to the right you get the following results.

MON	TUE	WED	THU	FRI	SAT
$ 6,182	$ 6,023	$ 6,253	$ 6,423	$ 5,418	$ 4,473

NOTE: If you just change "function number" 1 in the formula to the number 9 you will get the sum for the day instead of the average. Write the following formula in B13 and drag it to the right

=SUBTOTAL(9,B4:B12)

You will get the next results!

MON	TUE	WED	THU	FRI	SAT
$ 43,274	$ 42,163	$ 43,774	$ 44,958	$ 32,510	$ 31,312

Now try it in H4, try to get the Larger amount of income per each Hero (Function number for MAX is 4)

=SUBTOTAL(4,B4:G4)

Goku	$	8,826
Rocky Balboa	$	7,815
Obi Wan Kenobi	$	7,210
Jack Sparrow	$	9,351
Supergirl	$	6,652
Han Solo	$	9,662
Wolverine	$	9,958
Neo	$	9,063
Thor	$	8,090

That's how SUBTOTAL formula works! Try it by yourself by changing the "Function Numbers".

PRODUCT FUNCTION

WHAT IS THIS FUNCTION FOR?

Its main purpose is to multiply values in the cells you choose

WHICH IS THE MAIN BENEFIT OF THIS FORMULA?

You can multiply more than 2 values at the same time. All the values within the range will be multiplied.

HOW IS THIS FUNCTION STRUCTURED?

The syntax (Structure) of the **PRODUCT** function is the next one:

=PRODUCT(cell1,cell2,cell3,cell4,….)

Or

$$=PRODUCT(Cell1:Cell20)$$

WHAT DOES THAT MEAN?

You can multiply more than 2 values. You can insert the values as independent cells or as a range.

EXERCISE (Open file Chapter2ex9.xlsx)

Now let's learn this function trough an exercise. Let's find out how many dollars our heroes made last week.

Step 1: Star writing your formula in E4.

	WORK DAYS	**HOURS PER DAY**	**HOURLY WAGE**	
Goku	3	8	$	596

The most logical approach is to multiply Work Days times Hours per day times Hourly wage. You can do that by selecting each individual cell.

$$=PRODUCT(B4,C4,D4)$$

But you can also select the whole range

$$=PRODUCT(B4:D4)$$

Step 2: Press Enter and drag the formula down.

	WORK DAYS	HOURS PER DAY	HOURLY WAGE	
Goku	3	8	$ 596	$ 14,304
Rocky Balboa	4	6	$ 840	$ 20,160
Obi Wan Kenobi	5	7	$ 780	$ 27,300
Jack Sparrow	6	5	$ 849	$ 25,470
Supergirl	2	6	$ 546	$ 6,552
Han Solo	4	7	$ 768	$ 21,504

			$	$
Wolverine	5	8	746	29,840
Neo	6	6	941	33,876
Thor	3	4	554	6,648

That's it, this formula is easy to understand!

SUMPRODUCT FUNCTION

WHAT IS THIS FUNCTION FOR?

Its main purpose is to sum the results AFTER it multiplied some values. So, the function performs numerous multiplications first, and after that it sums all the results

WHICH IS THE MAIN BENEFIT OF THIS FORMULA?

You instead of using PRODUCT and then SUM… you can use **SUMPRODUCT** instead.

HOW IS THIS FUNCTION STRUCTURED?

The syntax (Structure) of the **SUMPRODUCT** function is the next one:

=SUMPRODUCT(range1,range2,range3 …etc)

WHAT DOES THAT MEAN?

Suppose that you just have 2 VERTICAL RANGES. So Range 1 will have the numbers 3,4,5 and Range 2 will have 8,6,7.

RANGE 1   RANGE 2

3	8
4	6
5	7

1. The first value of Range 1 will be multiplied by the first value of Range 2 (3*8)
2. The second value of Range 1 will be multiplied by the second of Range 2 (4*6)
3. The third value of Range 1 will be multiplied by the third of Range 2 (5*7)
4. At the end, the formula will SUM the result of all those 3 multiplications. That would be 83

EXERCISE (Open file Chapter2ex10.xlsx)

Now let's try with an exercise! You need to calculate the total amount paid to our heroes during the week. To do that, you have all the information you need (Workdays, Hours per day and Hourly Wage)

	WORK DAYS	HOURS PER DAY	HOURLY WAGE
Goku	3	8	$ 596
Rocky Balboa	4	6	$ 840
Obi Wan Kenobi	5	7	$ ·780
Jack Sparrow	6	5	$ 849
Supergirl	2	6	$ 546
Han Solo	4	7	$ 768
Wolverine	5	8	$ 746
Neo	6	6	$ 941
Thor	3	4	$ 554

Step 1: Position yourself in cell **A3** and start writing the formula.

=SUMPRODUCT(

Step 2: REMEMBER that the first value of your Range 1 will be multiplied by the first values of Range 2 and 3. In that case, you need and HORIZONTAL MULTIPLICATION, therefore you will need VERTICAL RANGES!

TIP: With **SUMPRODUCT,** any time you need and horizontal calculation, you will use vertical ranges. Any time you need vertical calculation you will use horizontal ranges.

RANGE 1	RANGE 2	RANGE 3
3	8	$ 596
4	6	$ 840
5	7	$ 780
6	5	$ 849
2	6	$ 546
4	7	$ 768

5	8	$	746
6	6	$	941
3	4	$	554

Write the next formula and press enter:

=SUMPRODUCT(B4:B12,C4:C12,D4:D12)

Why? Excel will multiply the following:

- 3*8*596 =
- 4*6*840 =
- 5*7*780 =
- 6*5*780 =
- Etc..
- At the end, excel will sum every result

You will get this result:

$	185,654

ANOTHER EXERCISE ON THE SAME SPREADSHEET (Open file Chapter2ex10.xlsx)

Now let's try to do the same exercise but with vertical calculations:

Remember that when you have to perform vertical multiplications with sumproduct (3*8*596 for Goku, and so on) you will need Horizontal ranges

Step 1: Position yourself in cell **G3** and start writing the formula.

=SUMPRODUCT(

Step 2: Write the next formula and press enter:

=SUMPRODUCT(H4:P4,H5:P5,H6:P6)

You will get the same result because the values were the same, but now you know how to perform horizontal and vertical SUMPRODUCTS:

$	185,654

Congratulations!! You have finished the first section of Excel Functions Ninja, arithmetic operations!

QUICK CHAPTER SUMMARY:

- Arithmetic operations are the basic form of formulas in Excel.
- They are super useful
- You can save a lot of time with some of them

CHAPTER 3:

ABSOLUTE REFERENCES AND RANKING AND STATISTICS FUNCTIONS

Let's start with Ranking and Statistics functions. Don't worry about statics ones because they are basic ones, but very useful when working with numbers.

BUT BEFORE DOING THAT, YOU NEED TO UNDERSTANT HOW ABSOLUTE REFERENCES WORK! THEY ARE GOING TO BE VITAL FOR YOU.

WHY DIDN'T I EXPLAINED THEM

BEFORE? BECAUSE YOU NEEDED TO BE ABLE TO PERFORM ARITHMETIC FUNCTIONS BEFORE TRIYNG TO USE ABSOLUTE REFERENCES.

SO, PLEASE USE THIS "ABSOLUTE REFERENCE" TOPIC AS:

1) THE INTRODUCTION OF THESE CHAPTER
2) SOMETHING YOU ARE GOING TO USE IN EVERY FUNCTION WHEN NEEDED

WHAT IS AND ABSOLUTE REFERENCE?

An Absolute References is used to "fix" or "immobilize" one part of the formula. It's super useful when you need to drag.

You have noticed from the previous exercises that every time you drag the formula, the cells within the formula are repositioned too. If you drag it one cell to the right, all the cells within the formula are moved one cell to the right.

Now let's suppose that you want that some cells within the formula remain the same, that's when you use absolute references.

HOW CAN YOU USE ABSOLUTE REFERENCES?

To explain this easy, when you add "$" signs to the cells in the formula (at the time of writing the formula) you are stablishing the absolute reference:

=A1*B1   Is NOT an absolute reference

=$A$1*B1   IS an absolute reference (you need two "$" signs per absolute reference)

With the absolute reference you are ordering excel that if you drag the formula, the first multiplication factor in the formula will always be A1.

NOTE: TO ADD ABSOLUTE REFERENCES YOU CAN MANUALLY WRITE THEM OR USE THE SHORTCUTS

FOR MAC: CMD + T

FOR WINDOWS F4

Let's try with an exercise to understand this thing once and for all.

EXERCISE (Open file Chapter3ex0.xlsx) Yes, it is exercise zero.

Let's try to figure out the earnings multiplying the hours worked by the hourly wage.

HOURLY WAGE	$15.00

HERO	HOURS	EARNINGS
The Atom	1349	
X-Men	640	
Asterix	585	
Maximus	1918	
Conan	1634	
Ethan Hunt	996	

Step 1: Position yourself in **C6** to write the formula (The Atom earnings) and write a simple multiplication formula.

$$=B3*B6$$

That way we get 1349 times $15.00 = $20,235

HOURLY WAGE	$15.00

HERO	HOURS	EARNINGS
The Atom	1349	$ 20,235

Everything is OK for now…

Step 2: DRAG THE FORMULA DOWN! And you'll see what happens.

HOURLY WAGE	$15.00

HERO	HOURS	EARNINGS
The Atom	1349	$ 20,235
X-Men	640	$ -
Asterix	585	#¡VALOR!
Maximus	1918	$ 2,587,382
Conan	1634	$ 1,045,760

Suddenly, you get $0 for X-Men, you get an ERROR for Asterix and you get wrong values for the following heroes. Everything is a mess!

What happened?

	HERO	HOURS	EARNINGS
3	HOURLY WAGE	$15.00	
4			
5	HERO	HOURS	EARNINGS
6	The Atom	1349	$ 20,235
7	X-Men	640	$ -
8	Asterix	585	=B5*B8
9	Maximus	1918	$ 2,587,382

The formula was moved and now is performing B5*B8

	HERO	HOURS	EARNINGS
3	HOURLY WAGE	$15.00	
4			
5	HERO	HOURS	EARNINGS
6	The Atom	1349	$ 20,235
7	X-Men	640	$ -
8	Asterix	585	#¡VALOR!
9	Maximus	1918	$ 2,587,382
10	Conan	1634	=B7*B10
11	Ethan Hunt	996	$ 582,660

The formula is performing B7*B8

The formula was moved because you dragged it! And now is calculating the values based on wrong cells.

What we really want is that the formula ALWAYS multiplies the HOURLY WAGE, we want to "Immobilize" that cell within the formula with Absolute References.

Step 3: Let's go back and fix this mess with the absolute references. Position yourself AGAIN in C6 (The first formula that you wrote) and ADD the Absolute Reference to the HOURLY WAGE.

HOW?

Option 1: Double Click in the cell and manually write the $ signs.

Option 2: Double click in the cell, then click between the B and the 3, and press shortcut CMD+T for Mac or F4 for Windows.

=$B$3*B6

Now that you have the Absolute reference, you can drag the formula down!

HOURLY WAGE	$15.00

HERO	HOURS	EARNINGS
The Atom	1349	$ 20,235
X-Men	640	$ 9,600
Asterix	585	$ 8,775
Maximus	1918	$ 28,770
Conan	1634	$ 24,510
Ethan Hunt	996	$ 14,940

GREAT! You can see that everything is normal!

3	HOURLY WAGE	$15.00	
4			
5	HERO	HOURS	EARNINGS
6	The Atom	1349	$ 20,235
7	X-Men	640	=$B$3*B7

	HERO	HOURS	EARNINGS
3	HOURLY WAGE	$15.00	
4			
5	HERO	HOURS	EARNINGS
6	The Atom	1349	$ 20,235
7	X-Men	640	$ 9,600
8	Asterix	585	$ 8,775
9	Maximus	1918	=$B$3*B9

Also, note that the formula ALWAYS uses B3 (The hourly wage) because you have immobilized it with Absolute References!

Now try to solve the following exercises by yourself!

145

1	2	3	4	5	6	7	8	9

2	
3	
4	
5	
6	
7	
8	
9	

That is the way to use Absolute References. Sometimes they are not necessary, but sometimes you can't write a formula without using them, it will depend on the situation.

Let's continue with the formulas!

RANDBETWEEN FUNCTION

WHAT IS THIS FUNCTION FOR?

Its main purpose is to insert random numbers, between the limits you stablish.

WHICH IS THE MAIN BENEFIT OF THIS FORMULA?

You can use it whenever you need to perform a test with random numbers.

HOW IS THIS FUNCTION STRUCTURED?

The syntax (Structure) of the **RANDBETWEEN** function is the next one:

=RANDBETWEEN(lower limit, upper limit)

WHAT DOES THAT MEAN?

You will get random numbers between the lower and upper limit that you stablish.

EXERCISE (Open file Chapter3ex1.xlsx)

Imagine the president is deciding the city each hero will be responsible for, but he wants to decide that randomly, and you have 15 super heroes. Then you could use this function.

	Supergirl
	Han Solo
	Guardians of the Galaxy
	Neo
	Thor
	James Bond
	Etc etc etc etc

Step 1: Position yourself in A3 to start writing the formula:

=RANDBETWEEN(1,15)

Why? Because you want numbers between 1

to 15

Step 2: Drag the formula down! And that's it, now you have the random numbers.

NOTE: The numbers will change every time you close and open the file, so copy and paste them as plain values (TEXT)

MEDIAN FUNCTION

WHAT IS THIS FUNCTION FOR?

Its main purpose is to find the number that is right in the middle of a group of numbers

WHICH IS THE MAIN BENEFIT OF THIS FORMULA?

You can find the middle number (different from average)

HOW IS THIS FUNCTION STRUCTURED?

The syntax (Structure) of the **MEDIAN** function is the next one:

=MEDIAN(cell1,cell2,cell3,etc,etc)

Or

=MEDIAN(cell1:cel21)

WHAT DOES THAT MEAN?

You will get the middle number within the group of cells you stablish. You can use ranges.

EXERCISE (Open file Chapter3ex2.xlsx)

You have the last year's income of each super hero, try to find the middle number. You have 15 superheroes so the middle number would be the 8th.

	MEDIAN
$ 460,927	Supergirl
$ 598,596	Han Solo
$ 328,880	Guardians of the Galaxy
$ 757,124	Neo
$ 651,958	Etc, etc, etc

Step 1: Position yourself in A3 to start writing the formula. Remember that the range you are going to use is the one with the incomes.

$$=MEDIAN(A4:A18)$$

That way you get the result.

$ 460,927	**MEDIAN**

You found the median income. Now you know that SUPERGIRL is the one that earned the middle income the last year.

Additionally, if you use the AVERAGE function you will notice that it is not the same number. The MEDIAN is the middle number, while the AVERAGE is gotten by adding every number and then dividing the total between the number of participants.

NOTE: YOU CAN TRY CREATING RANDOM NUMBERS WITH RANDBETWEEN AND WATCH HOW THE MEDIAN CHANGES.

MODE FUNCTION

WHAT IS THIS FUNCTION FOR?

Its main purpose is to find the most repetitive number within a group of numbers.

WHICH IS THE MAIN BENEFIT OF THIS FORMULA?

You can find patterns or most popular numbers within a group to make decisions

HOW IS THIS FUNCTION STRUCTURED?

The syntax (Structure) of the **MODE** function is the next one:

=MODE(cell1,cell2,cell3,etc,etc)

Or

=MODE(cell1:cel21)

WHAT DOES THAT MEAN?

You will get the most repetitive number within the group of cells you stablish. You can use ranges.

EXERCISE (Open file Chapter3ex3.xlsx)

You have the number of lives saved by each hero during the last hour! Your job is to find the most repetitive number of lives saved.

	MODE
1	Supergirl
1	Han Solo
2	Guardians of the Galaxy
3	Etc etc etc

Step 1: Position yourself in A3 to start writing the formula. Remember that the range you are going to use is the one with the incomes.

$$=MODE(A4:A18)$$

That way you get the result.

3	**MODE**

Now you know that the most common for a hero is to save 3 lives within an hour. But Supergirl and Han Solo are not that good at that.

NOTE: YOU CAN TRY CREATING RANDOM NUMBERS WITH RANDBETWEEN AND WATCH HOW THE MODE CHANGES

LARGE FUNCTION

WHAT IS THIS FUNCTION FOR?

Its main purpose is to sort the numbers, and find the "N" greater number that you want to find

WHICH IS THE MAIN BENEFIT OF THIS FORMULA?

You can modify the formula to find the number you want to find based on your criteria.

HOW IS THIS FUNCTION STRUCTURED?

The syntax (Structure) of the **LARGE** function is the next one:

=LARGE(range,number)

WHAT DOES THAT MEAN?

If you write 1 in the second argument (number) you will get the larger number within the range, but if you write 2 you will get the 2nd larger number, if you write 3 you will get the 3rd larger and so on.

EXERCISE (Open file Chapter3ex4.xlsx)

You have the number of missions made by our heroes, and we need to find the number 1, 3, 5, and 10 according to the number of missions they have completed.

TOP # OF MISSIONS
1
3
5
7
10

Step 1: Position yourself in **F4** and start writing the formula

=LARGE(

Step 2: Select the Range for the missions, that is **B4:B58**. But wait! **REMEMBER THE ABSOLUTE REFERENCES? YOU**

WILL NEED TO ADD THEM NOW IN BOTH PARTS OF THE RANGE IN ORDER TO IMMOVILZE THAT SECTON OF THE FORMULA.

=LARGE($B$4:$B$54,

Step 3: Select the number that you are looking for. To make it easier I wrote the numbers in a table so you can select **E4** (without absolute references because we want that value to move as we drag the formula down)

=LARGE($B$4:$B$54,E4)

Step 4: Drag the formula down!

TOP # OF MISSIONS	
1	1988
3	1939
5	1918
7	1859

10   1812

Now you have the values that you want! And if you chance the numbers you will see that the values automatically are modified!

SMALL FUNCTION

WHAT IS THIS FUNCTION FOR?

Its main purpose is to sort the numbers, and find the "N" lower number that you want to find. This function is actually the opposite of the LARGE Function, so it works almost the same.

WHICH IS THE MAIN BENEFIT OF THIS FORMULA?

You can modify the formula to find the

number you want to find based on your criteria.

HOW IS THIS FUNCTION STRUCTURED?

The syntax (Structure) of the **SMALL** function is the next one:

=SMALL(range,number)

WHAT DOES THAT MEAN?

If you write 1 in the second argument (number) you will get the lower number within the range, but if you write 2 you will get the 2nd lower number, if you write 3 you will get the 3rd lower and so on.

EXERCISE (Open file Chapter3ex5.xlsx)

You have the number of missions made by our heroes, and we need to find the bottom 1, 3, 5, and 10 according to the number of missions they have completed.

BOTTOM	# OF MISSIONS
1	
3	
5	
7	
10	

Step 1: Position yourself in **F4** and start writing the formula

=SMALL(

Step 2: Select the Range for the missions, that is **B4:B58**. But wait! REMEMBER THE ABSOLUTE REFERENCES? YOU WILL NEED TO ADD THEM NOW IN BOTH PARTS OF THE RANGE IN ORDER TO IMMOVILZE THAT

SECTON OF THE FORMULA.

$$=SMALL(\$B\$4:\$B\$54,$$

Step 3: Select the number that you are looking for, it is in **E4** (without absolute references because we want that value to move as we drag the formula down)

$$=SMALL(\$B\$4:\$B\$54,E4)$$

Step 4: Drag the formula down!

BOTTOM	# OF MISSIONS
1	532
3	593
5	640
7	659
10	877

Now you have the values that you want! And

if you chance the numbers you will see that the values automatically are modified!

RANK FUNCTION

WHAT IS THIS FUNCTION FOR?

Its main purpose is to rank the values within a range. It writes the number 1 for the Top value.

WHICH IS THE MAIN BENEFIT OF THIS FORMULA?

Easily get the ranking of a set of values.

HOW IS THIS FUNCTION STRUCTURED?

The syntax (Structure) of the **RANK** function is the next one:

$$=RANK(number,array)$$

WHAT DOES THAT MEAN?

The first argument must be the value to rank and the Array is the range of values (Remember to add Absolute references if you need to drag the formula)

EXERCISE (Open file Chapter3ex6.xlsx)

Our heroes are unemployed because of the COVID-19 crisis, so they needed to go out and sale some items, but obviously the suck at selling. Your job is to rank them.

HERO	ITEMS SOLD	RANKING
Krillin	6	
Aragorn	23	
Zorro	23	

Black Panther	11	

Step 1: Position yourself in C4 and start writing the formula:

$$=RANK($$

Step 2: Select the number to Rank (Items sold by Krillin) B4. And the Range where all the values are. Remember to add Absolute references to the range.

$$=RANK(B4,\$B\$4:\$B\$24)$$

Step 3: Drag the formula down and there you have!!

HERO	ITEMS SOLD	RANKING
Krillin	6	20
Aragorn	23	2
Zorro	23	2
Black Panther	11	15

Catwoman	16	11

IMPORTANT NOTE: Look at Aragorn and Zorro, they sold the same amount of items and the ranking for both of them is 2. This means that the RANK formula WILL OMIT THE NUMBER 3 RANK.

HERO	ITEMS SOLD	RANKING
Vegeta	24	1
Aragorn	23	2
Zorro	23	2
Ant-Man	21	4
Doctor Strange	20	5
Wonder Woman	20	5
Incredible Hulk	20	5
Hellboy	19	8

Here you can see what I'm talking about,

there are 2 numbers 2, and 3 numbers 5 tied. So, the Rank formula doesn't show ranks 3, 6 nor 7.

RANK.AVG FUNCTION

WHAT IS THIS FUNCTION FOR?

If you want some kind of more exact ranking, this would do it. Its main purpose is to rank the values within a range. It writes the number 1 for the Top value. But it also AVERAGES the tied rankings.

WHICH IS THE MAIN BENEFIT OF THIS FORMULA?

Easily get the ranking of a set of values and AVERAGES the tied rankings.

HOW IS THIS FUNCTION STRUCTURED?

The syntax (Structure) of the **RANK.AVG** function is the next one:

$$=RANK.AVG(number,array)$$

WHAT DOES THAT MEAN?

The first argument must be the value to rank and the Array is the range of values (Remember to add Absolute references if you need to drag the formula).

EXERCISE (Open file Chapter3ex7.xlsx)

Let's take a similar exercise to the previous. You will need to RANK the heroes again, but now with RANK.AVG

HERO	ITEMS SOLD	RANKING

Krillin	6	
Aragorn	23	
Zorro	23	
Black Panther	11	

Step 1: Position yourself in C4 and start writing the formula:

=RANK.AVG(

Step 2: Select the number to Rank (Items sold by Krillin) B4. And the Range where all the values are. Remember to add Absolute references to the range.

=RANK.AVG(B4,$B$4:$B$24)

Step 3: Drag the formula down and there you have!! But now watch the differences.

HERO	ITEMS SOLD	RANKING

Vegeta	24	1
Aragorn	23	2.5
Zorro	23	2.5
Ant-Man	21	4
Doctor Strange	20	6
Wonder Woman	20	6
Incredible Hulk	20	6
Hellboy	19	8
Sarah Connor	18	9

Note that Aragorn and Zorro now get a Ranking of 2.5, Why? Because they are Ranking 2 and 3 and the average of 2 and 3 is 2.5

Also note that Doctor Strange, Wonder Woman, and Incredible Hulk have a Ranking of 6 instead of 5. Why? While the RANK formula assigns the higher Rank for all of them (5) the RANK.AVG average their ranks (5,6,7) and assigns the average value (6) which is more realistic.

Imagine you have 10 heroes with 24 sales. It would be unrealistic to have 10 number one rankings! That is what this RANK.AVG formula is used for.

ROUND FUNCTION

WHAT IS THIS FUNCTION FOR?

Super useful formula to decide the number of digits you want. Its main purpose is to round a number matching the number of digits you stablish

WHICH IS THE MAIN BENEFIT OF

THIS FORMULA?

Easily get a rounded number according to what you need.

HOW IS THIS FUNCTION STRUCTURED?

The syntax (Structure) of the **ROUND** function is the next one:

=ROUND(number,digits)

WHAT DOES THAT MEAN?

The first argument must be the number you want to round (The cell), and the second argument must be the number of digits that you want (It also can be a cell)

Let's take a look at how this formula works. The number we want to round is in the left column, the number of digits we want is in the middle column and the result we would get is in the right column.

NUMBER	DIGITS	RESULT
3.456	0	**3**
3.456	1	**3.5**
3.456	2	**3.46**
3.456	3	**3.456**
76456	-1	**76460**
76456	-2	**76500**
76456	-3	**76000**
76456	-4	**80000**

NOTE 1: The number 3.456 rounded with 0 digits is 3, Why? Because the surplus fraction .456 is closer to the 3.000 than to the 4.000, and we want 0 digits so the result is 3.

NOTE 2: The number 3.456 rounded with 1 digit is 3.5, Why? Because the surplus fraction .456 is closer to the 3.500 than to the 3.400, and we want 1 digit so the result is 3.5

NOTE 3: The number 3.456 rounded with 2 digits is 3.46, Why? Because the surplus fraction ..45_6_ is closer to the 3.460 than to the 3.450, and we want 2 digits so the result is 3.46

NOTE 4 (negative rounded): The number 76456 rounded with -1 digits is 76460, Why? Because the surplus fraction 7645_6_ is closer to the 76460 than to the 76450, and we want -1 digits so the result is 76460. (-1 is equal to rounding to the closest 10)

NOTE 5 (negative rounded): The number 76456 rounded with -4 digits is 80000, Why? Because the surplus fraction 7_6456_ is closer to the 80000 than to the 70000, and we want -4 digits so the result is 80000. (-4 is equal to rounding to the closest 10000)

You get the idea! So now let's go to the

exercise

EXERCISE (Open file Chapter3ex8.xlsx)

I have already explained you how this formula works, so now try to solve the exercise. You can use the number above each column as the digit for the formula, or you can write it manually in the formula.

		1	0
HERO	**NUMBER**	**ROUND 1**	**ROUND 0**
Krillin	210.7879		
Aragorn	278.7500		
Zorro	203.7500		
Black Panther	192.6389		

Step 1: Position yourself in C4 and write the first formula

=ROUND(B4,1)

NOTE: If you want to use the number 1 (the cell) above each column remember to add Absolute References like this

$$=ROUND(B4,\$C\$2)$$

Step 2: Drag the formula down and repeat the process for each column.

ROUNDUP FUNCTION

WHAT IS THIS FUNCTION FOR?

This is a variant of ROUND. Its main purpose is to round a number matching the number of digits you stablish BUT ALWAYS UP! Not down.

WHICH IS THE MAIN BENEFIT OF THIS FORMULA?

Easily get a rounded number according

to what you need, but the rounding will be always up.

HOW IS THIS FUNCTION STRUCTURED?

The syntax (Structure) of the **ROUNDUP** function is the next one:

=ROUNDUP(number,digits)

WHAT DOES THAT MEAN?

The first argument must be the number you want to round (The cell), and the second argument must be the number of digits that you want (It also can be a cell)

Let's take a look at how this formula works. You will find something different from the ROUND formula. You will notice that it doesn't matter the closeness of the number, you will always round to the closest number UP.

NUMBER	DIGITS	RESULT
3.111	0	**4**
3.111	1	**3.2**
3.111	2	**3.12**
3.111	3	**3.111**
11123	-1	**11130**
11123	-2	**11200**
11123	-3	**12000**
11123	-4	**20000**

NOTE 1: The number 3.111 with 0 digits of rounding will go up to 4

NOTE 2: The number 11123 with -2 digits in rounding (the closest 100) will go up to 11200. It doesn't matter that 11123 is closest to 11100. The formula will round that up to the closest hundred.

NOTE 3: The number 11123 with -4 digits in rounding (the closest 10000) will go up to 20000. It doesn't matter that 11123 is closest to 10000. The formula will round that up to the closest ten thousand.

EXERCISE (Open file Chapter3ex9.xlsx)

I have already explained you how this formula works, so now try to solve the exercise. You can use the number above each column as the digit for the formula, or you can write it manually in the formula.

If you have any doubts you can watch the answer key within the spreadsheet.

HERO	NUMBER	ROUND 1	ROUND 0
Krillin	20446.4242		
Aragorn	27038.7500		
Zorro	19763.7500		

| Black Panther | 18685.9722 | | |
| Catwoman | 30188.2188 | | |

ROUNDDOWN FUNCTION

WHAT IS THIS FUNCTION FOR?

This is a variant of ROUNDUP. Its main purpose is to round a number matching the number of digits you stablish BUT ALWAYS DOWN! Not up.

WHICH IS THE MAIN BENEFIT OF THIS FORMULA?

Easily get a rounded number according to what you need, but the rounding will be always down.

HOW IS THIS FUNCTION STRUCTURED?

The syntax (Structure) of the **ROUNDDOWN** function is the next one:

=ROUNDDOWN(number,digits)

WHAT DOES THAT MEAN?

The first argument must be the number you want to round (The cell), and the second argument must be the number of digits that you want (It also can be a cell)

Let's take a look at how this formula works. You will find something different from the ROUNDUP formula. You will notice that it doesn't matter the closeness of the number, you will always round to the closest number DOWN.

NUMBER	DIGITS	RESULT

3.789	0	**3**
3.789	1	**3.7**
3.789	2	**3.78**
3.789	3	**3.789**
18678	-1	**18670**
18678	-2	**18600**
18678	-3	**18000**
18678	-4	**10000**

This ROUNDDOWN formula works exactly the same as the ROUNDUP formula with the only difference that it rounds everything down. But the DIGIT mechanics work the same.

EXERCISE (Open file Chapter3ex10.xlsx)

I have already explained you how this formula works, so now try to solve the exercise. You can use the number above each column as the digit for the formula, or you can write it manually in the formula.

If you have any doubts you can watch the answer key.

HERO	NUMBER	ROUND 1	ROUND 0
Krillin	20446.4242		
Aragorn	27038.7500		
Zorro	19763.7500		
Black Panther	18685.9722		
Catwoman	30188.2188		

CONVERT FUNCTION

WHAT IS THIS FUNCTION FOR?

Its main purpose is to convert any

measure to another kind of measure. For example, pounds to grams, or miles to yards or meters.

WHICH IS THE MAIN BENEFIT OF THIS FORMULA?

Easily get a calculator to convert any measures you want.

HOW IS THIS FUNCTION STRUCTURED?

The syntax (Structure) of the **CONVERT** function is the next one:

=CONVERT(number,from,to)

WHAT DOES THAT MEAN?

The first argument must be the number you want to round (The cell). In the second argument you must select the input measure. In the third argument you must select the output measure that you want.

EXERCISE (Open file Chapter3ex11.xlsx)

In this exercise you have the weight and speed of every hero. The weight is in pound and the speed is in miles.

HERO	POUNDS	MILES/HOUR	GRAMS	YARDS	METERS
Krillin	182	36			
Aragorn	260	39			
Zorro	325	46			
Black Panther	309	35			
Catwoman	222	30			

Your job is to convert the POUNDS to GRAMS and the MILES to YARDS and METERS.

Step 1: Position yourself to write the firs formula in **E4**. Then start writing and select the first number that you want to convert (The weight of Krillin)

$$=CONVERT(B4,$$

Step 2: Now, you have to select the input measure, POUNDS. So, select "lbm"

$$=CONVERT(B4,"lbm",$$

Step 3: Now, you have to select the output measure, GRAMS. So, select "g", close the parenthesis and press Enter. Then drag the formula down.

$$=CONVERT(B4,"lbm","g")$$

GRAMS YARDS METERS

GRAMS	YARDS	METERS
82554		
117934		
147418		

Now it is your turn to complete the YARDS and the METERS section!

CONGRATULATIONS! THIS IS THE END OF THIS CHAPTER!

NOW IT IS TIME TO CONTINUE WITH THE SEARCH AND REFERENCE FORMULAS IN ORDER FOR YOU TO BECOME AN EXCEL FORMULAS NINJA!

QUICK CHAPTER SUMMARY:

- Absolute References are sometimes necessary to drag the formulas.
- Statistics formulas are widely used to rank, round and get the most repetitive numbers

Are you enjoying this book?

Do you think it's easy to understand?

Have the exercises helped you learn faster?

Without knowing your opinion I won't know if the book has helped you to become a better Excel user.

You can share your thoughts with me by writing a Review

CHAPTER 4

SEARCH AND REFERENCE FORMULAS

Now is the time to talk about one of the most important formulas in Excel, the Search and Reference formulas. In order to become and Excel Formulas Champion you need to master at least 2 formulas in this section.

These formulas are widely used because of their ability to save time with databases. The 3 formulas that we are going to explore are:

- VLOOKUP
- HLOOKUP
- XLOOKUP

Let's start!

VLOOKUP FUNCTION

WHAT IS THIS FUNCTION FOR?

To make this simple, this formula is the most used in Excel. It is used to obtain values (related to a reference cell) from a big database without having to find them manually.

WHICH IS THE MAIN BENEFIT OF THIS FORMULA?

You can easily find and relate info from a database in order to match the info that you are looking for. You'll understand it better with the exercise.

HOW IS THIS FUNCTION STRUCTURED?

The syntax (Structure) of the **VLOOKUP** function is the next one:

=VLOOKUP(lookup value, lookup array, column, range lookup)

WHAT DOES THAT MEAN?

LOOKUP VALUE: Is the base Value that you already know. Excel will try to find that value in a database and return another value (in another column) that matches your lookup value

LOOKUP ARRAY: Is the range where the data base is located

COLUMN: Is the Column number (of the database) where your desired result is located. If you want to get the result from the 2nd column in the database, you will need to write 2 in this argument.

RANGE LOOKUP: This is optional, normally you want to use "0" because that means you want an EXACT MATCH. This way Excel will only find values that match exactly with your LOOKUP VALUE.

Let's try an exercise for you to understand it better.

EXERCISE (Open file Chapter4ex1.xlsx)

Now you have an ID search cell and some info that you need to pull out of a database. To your right you have a big data base with the information in random order.

ID	HEROE	SECTOR	CITY
1	The Atom	Healthcare	Danvers, Massachusetts
2	X-Men	Utilities	Canonsburg, Pennsylvania

	Industrial	North Chicago,
3 Asterix	Goods	Illinois

DATA BASE

Due to the COVID crisis, with no wars and no violence, our heroes needed to start working in some companies (although it was hard for them to get a job). Each one of them has an ID assigned. We need to build a tool to search the whole information by just changing the ID.

ID	HEROE
14	
22	
56	

SEARCH TOOL

IMPORTANT NOTE:

Notice that we have 1 piece of information

that matches in our Search Tool and in our Database. That piece of information is the **ID NUMBER**, so what we need to do is to use that **ID NUMBER** as an **ANCHOR** value (Lookup Value) to grab the other values that we need (The name of the hero)

Step 1: Please start writing the formula at **B3**, to get the first hero name.

=VLOOKUP(

Step 2: The 1st argument (The lookup value) is our "anchor value", the value that we have in both tables, the ID NUMBER. So select the corresponding cell. In this case is first the cell with an ID number in our search tool, **A3**

=VLOOKUP(A3,

Why? Because Excel will try to find in the database whatever we have in **A3** (in this case, excel will try to find in the database the number 14)

Step 3: Select the Lookup Array (The database) in order to indicate excel where to search. Remember to add ABSOLUTE REFERENCES in order to be able to drag the formula later.

$$=VLOOKUP(A3,\$F\$2:\$J\$89,$$

Why? Because the database starts in F2 and ends in J89.

SUPER IMPORTANT NOTE:

IN ORDER FOR VLOOKUP TO WORK CORRECTLY, THE FIRST COLUMN IN THE DATABASE MUST HAVE YOUR LOOKUP VALUE (ANCHOR VALUE). IN OTHER WORDS, IF YOU ARE USING THE ID NUMBER AS YOUR LOOKUP VALUE, THE ID NUMBER MUST BE IN THE FIRST COLUMN (LEFT COLUMN) OF YOUR DATABASE.

Step 3: Write the column number where your desired result is. In this example, your desired result is the name of the hero, so, IN YOUR DATABASE the name of the hero is in the 2nd Column, then you need to write 2.

=VLOOKUP(A3,$F$2:$J$89,2

Step 3: Write 0, in order to get and EXACT search. Close and drag the formula.

=VLOOKUP(A3,$F$2:$J$89,2,0)

ID	HEROE
14	Optimus Prime
22	Catwoman
56	Fantastic Four
70	Rocky Balboa
80	Gandalf

That's it! Look how fast you got the names of the heroes using their IDs, and if you change the ID number the name will change too! Try it.

ID	HEROE
20	Zorro
30	Doc Savage
40	Luke Skywalker

Now try by yourself to fill the search tool completely!

ID	HEROE	CITY	BOSS
14	Optimus Prime		
22	Catwoman		
56	Fantastic Four		
70	Rocky Balboa		
80	Gandalf		

BY THE WAY, VLOOKUP IS A SUPER USEFUL FORMULA, IT WILL TAKE MUCH MORE THAN THIS TO

MASTER IT. SO I WOULD REALLY ENCOURAGE YOU TO GET MY "EXCEL VLOOKUP CHAMPION" BOOK. IT IS A FULL BOOK GETTING DEEP INTO THIS VLOOKUP FUNCTION!

"THE ONLY EXCEL VLOOKUP FUNCTION BOOK YOU WILL EVER NEED" - Sales Manager of an Oil Products Manufacturing Company

HLOOKUP FUNCTION

WHAT IS THIS FUNCTION FOR?

This formula is the brother formula of VLOOKUP. While Vlookup works vertically, HLOOKUP WARKS HORIZONTALLY. So you don't get the column, YOU GET THE ROW THAT YOU WANT.

WHICH IS THE MAIN BENEFIT OF THIS FORMULA?

You can easily find and relate info from a database in order to match the info that you are looking for.

HOW IS THIS FUNCTION STRUCTURED?

The syntax (Structure) of the **HLOOKUP** function is the next one:

=HLOOKUP(lookup value, lookup array, ROW, range lookup)

WHAT DOES THAT MEAN?

LOOKUP VALUE: Is the base Value that you already know. Excel will try to find that value in a database and return another value (in another row) that matches your lookup value

LOOKUP ARRAY: Is the range where the data base is located

ROW: Is the ROW number (of the database) where your desired result is located. If you want to get the result from the 2nd ROW in the database, you will need to write 2 in this argument.

RANGE LOOKUP: This is optional, normally you want to use "0" because that means you want an EXACT MATCH. This way Excel will only find values that match exactly with your LOOKUP VALUE.

Let's try an exercise.

EXERCISE (Open file Chapter4ex2.xlsx)

Now let's try with a similar exercise than the previous but with a horizontal database

ID	1	2	3
HEROE	The Atom	X-Men	Asterix
SECTOR	Healthcare	Utilities	Industrial Goods

You will need to create the same Search Tool but now the database is horizontal.

Step 1: Please start writing the formula at **B3**, to get the first hero name.

=HLOOKUP(

Step 2: The 1st argument (The lookup value) is our "anchor value", the value that we have in both tables, the ID NUMBER. So, select the corresponding cell. In this case is first the cell with an ID number in our search tool, **A3**

$$=HLOOKUP(A3,$$

Step 3: Select the Lookup Array (The database) in order to indicate excel where to search. Remember to add ABSOLUTE REFERENCES in order to be able to drag the formula later.

$$=HLOOKUP(A3,\$G\$2:\$CP\$6,$$

Why? Because the database starts in G2 and ends in CP6.

SUPER IMPORTANT NOTE:

IN ORDER FOR HLOOKUP TO WORK CORRECTLY, THE FIRST ROW IN THE DATABASE MUST HAVE YOUR LOOKUP VALUE (ANCHOR VALUE). IN OTHER WORDS, IF YOU ARE USING THE ID NUMBER AS YOUR

LOOKUP VALUE, THE ID NUMBER MUST BE IN THE FIRST ROW (UPPER ROW) OF YOUR DATABASE.

Step 3: Write the row number where your desired result is. In this example, your desired result is the name of the hero, so, IN YOUR DATABASE the name of the hero is in the 2nd ROW, then you need to write 2.

=HLOOKUP(A3,$G$2:$CP$6,2

Step 3: Write 0, in order to get and EXACT search. Close and drag the formula.

=HLOOKUP(A3,$G$2:$CP$6,2,0)

ID	HEROE
14	Optimus Prime
22	Catwoman
56	Fantastic Four
70	Rocky Balboa

80	Gandalf

There you go! You have the correct results! Now try to solve the remaining part of the exercise by yourself. Remember that the main difference is that when using HLOOKUP you will need the ROW, not the column.

XLOOKUP FUNCTION

Important note: Depending on the time you are reading this, you may need to use "EXCEL ON THE WEB" to use this formula. Or maybe you already have it incorporated in your Office 365 subscription.

WHAT IS THIS FUNCTION FOR?

This one is the newest formula from the Microsoft Excel's Team, and it is so great! It is like the big brother of VLOOKUP. Vlookup has one big limitation in the first column (left column) you need to have your lookup value, that makes it unable to search from right to left.

But with Xlookup that problem is gone! XLOOKUP can search from right to left, without any problems!

WHICH IS THE MAIN BENEFIT OF THIS FORMULA?

You can easily overcome the limitations of Vlookup

HOW IS THIS FUNCTION STRUCTURED?

The syntax (Structure) of the **XLOOKUP** function is the next one:

=XLOOKUP(lookup value, search array, return array, if not found)

WHAT DOES THAT MEAN?

LOOKUP VALUE: Same thing as Vlookup and Hlookup

SEARCH ARRAY: This is the Range where excel is going to search for your lookup value.

RETURN ARRAY: Once Excel has found the lookup value in the search array, Excel is going to return the value that is in the return array.

IMPORTANT NOTE: Notice that here we have two ARRAYS (Ranges). One is to search the lookup value and another is to return a result. While in Vlookup and Hlookup we had 1 Array and we need to write a number (column number or row number) to get a result.

Because of this, you won't need to count the columns or the rows, you just need to select the correct RETURN ARRAY.

IF NOT FOUND: This is optional, you can write something just in case Excel doesn't find the Lookup Value

Let's try an exercise.

EXERCISE (Open file Chapter4ex3.xlsx)

A similar Exercise than the previous with Vlookup, but the main difference is that we have the IDs to the right! This would be hard for Vlookup, but it is easy for Xlookup.

HEROE	SECTOR	BOSS	ID
Ethan Hunt	Utilities	Janel Joplin	6
Tsunade	Technology	Cristin Hogans	7
Aquaman	Conglomerates	Kenia Tandy	8
Ben-Hur	Healthcare	Fairy Beauchemin	9

Step 1: Please start writing the formula at **B3**, to get the first hero name.

$$=XLOOKUP($$

Step 2: The 1st argument (The lookup value) is our "anchor value", the value that we have in both tables, the ID NUMBER. So, select the corresponding cell. In this case is first the cell with an ID number in our search tool, **A3**

$$=XLOOKUP(A3,$$

Step 3: HERE COMES THE BIG DIFFERENCE. Now, you need to select the SEARCH ARRAY, in other words, the range WITHIN THE DATABASE where the ID numbers are (and add Absolute references)

$$=XLOOKUP(A3,\$J\$2:\$J\$89$$

Why? Because the IDs are in J2:J89.

Step 4: HERE COMES ANOTHER BIG DIFFERENCE. Now, you need to select the RETURN ARRA, in other words, the range WITHIN THE DATABASE where the Names of the heroes are (and add Absolute references). Remember, you just need to select the column where the names of the heroes are.

=XLOOKUP(A3,$J$2:$J$89,$F$2:$F$89,

Why? Because all the names of the heroes are in F2:F89

Step 5: Write "not found" in the 4th argument, just in case Excel doesn't find an ID number. Close the formula, press enter and drag it down.

=XLOOKUP(A3,$J$2:$J$89,$F$2:$F$89,"n ot found")

ID	HEROE
10	Black Canary
30	Doc Savage
50	Loki

70	Rocky Balboa
90	not found

Notice that the ID 90 was not found because it doesn't exist.

Now try to do the same for to complete the exercise. You will need to get the following results to consider it correct.

ID	HEROE	CITY	BOSS
10	Black Canary	Raleigh, North Carolina	Deadra Hammersley
30	Doc Savage	Pasadena, California	Tabetha Galloway
50	Loki	Norwalk, Connecticut	Myles Probst
70	Rocky Balboa	Denver, Colorado	Conchita Benford
90	not found	not found	not found

BY THE WAY, XLOOKUP IS A SUPER USEFUL FORMULA, IT WILL TAKE MUCH MORE THAN THIS TO MASTER IT. SO I WOULD REALLY ENCOURAGE YOU TO GET MY RECENTLY RELEASED "EXCEL XLOOKUP CHAMPION" BOOK.

YOU WILL LEARN TO USE EVERY SINGLE DETAIL OF THIS AWESOME FORMULA!

"THIS NEW FORMULA MAKES IT EVEN EASIER THAN EXCEL VLOOKUP FUNCTION" - Manager of a Retail Chain Store

This is the end of this Chapter! You are now even closer of being an Excel Formulas Ninja!

Let's keep moving forward, we still have some great formulas to learn!

QUICK CHAPTER SUMMARY:

- Search and Reference formulas are super useful
- They involve a Results Table (Search Tool) and a Database from where you need to pull out the info that you want.
- Vlookup is the most used. Xlookup is the most flexible.

CHAPTER 5

FINANCIAL FORMULAS

Now, we are going to learn to use some financial formulas for your day to day life. This section may be a little bit difficult if you don't have financial background, but I'll do my best to explain all the concepts in plain English.

However, I'm not going to include here super complex financial formulas because that is not the objective of this section. What I am going to do is to show you how to use the formulas that will make a difference in your day to day life and in your work. Let's start!

(Disclaimer: If you are a financial analyst or work in a finance department chances are that you already know this formulas)

NPV FUNCTION

WHAT IS THIS FUNCTION FOR?

Technically, the NET PRESENT VALUE formula is used to **"discount"** a series of incoming cashflows after making an investment. The normal discount factor may be the **inflation or the risk-free 10 year Treasury Bond.**

<u>Plain English of "DISCOUNTING" for non-Financial guys:</u>

You already know that the cost of the goods and services rises every year, this "force" is called "inflation". Because of inflation if you need to buy "X" product today it may cost $100, but if you wait till next year it may cost $103. That's a difference of 3 dollars, that's 3% of inflation on that year.

Because of that, there is something called "The value of money over time" that says: "Money is worth more NOW than later, because you can buy more things NOW than later, because later you will need to pay with inflation"

So, what happens when you INVEST in a business/stock TODAY a large sum of money, and each year you are going have cashflow coming in to your pocket? You will need to account for that inflation! Because if you get $100 of cashflow 5 years from now, those $100 in 5 years can buy less thing than $100 NOW.

When you DISCOUNT your future cashflows and take them back to the present, you get the NET PRESENT VALUE, in other words, you get the EQUIVALENT PURCHASING POWER of today's money.

HOW CAN YOU USE A DISCOUNT FACTOR?

Use the higher of these two options:

Option 1: Use the average inflation of your country

Option 2: Use the 10 Year Treasury Bond of your country. It is also called risk-free rate.

Why? The higher the discount rate, the more you allow yourself for error in your valuation.

WHICH IS THE MAIN BENEFIT OF THIS FORMULA?

You can easily discover the NET PRESENT VALUE

HOW IS THIS FUNCTION STRUCTURED?

The syntax (Structure) of the **NPV** function is the next one

=NPV(rate,value1,value2,etc)

WHAT DOES THAT MEAN?

RATE: Is the discount factor (the inflation or the risk-free rate)

VALUES: This is the Range of the values

IMPORTANT NOTE: The firs value MUST be negative because it is supposed to be an investment (expense) so the money is going OUT.

Let's try an exercise.

EXERCISE (Open file Chapter5ex1.xlsx)

Every hero is trying to get the most of their money, so they are going to install solar panels at their home (this could be you investing money in your home or in any equipment). They were told that their investment will pay by itself in 5 YEARS once the solar panels are installed.

So, let's try to figure that out.

IRON MAN invested $40,000 in the period 0 (That's where we need the negative number). And then, he get the following savings (as cashflow coming in to his pocket because it was not going out of his pocket)

IRON
MAN

PERIOD	CASHFLOW
0	-40000
1	10000
2	12000

3	9000
4	10000
5	13000

Step 1: Position yourself in E5 and start writing the formula

$$=NPV($$

Step 2: Select the discount rate (the inflation cell) E3

$$=NPV(E3,$$

Step 3: Select the range of EVERY CASHFLOW (including the investment), close the parenthesis and press enter.

$$=NPV(E3,B4:B9)$$

IRON MAN

PERIOD	CASHFLOW	INFLATION	
0	-40000		4%

1	10000
2	12000
3	9000
4	10000
5	13000

NPV	$7,638.58

Notice that, with that invested amount and those savings, the investment did pay off in 5 years.

TAKING INTO ACCOUNT THE INFLATION OF 4% Iron Man gets a positive cashflow of $7,638 in TODAY'S MONEY (The equivalent to today's PURCHASING POWER)

If you simply SUM you will get a VALUE of $14,000 positive. But that doesn't take into account the inflation.

Now do the same for the remaining super heroes and discover if their investments pad off.

XNPV FUNCTION

WHAT IS THIS FUNCTION FOR?

This is the enhanced version of NPV. The main difference is that NPV formula only accepts 1 cashflow per year and it calculates each cashflow with an exact separation of 1 year.

But what happens if (as it normally happens) you get more cashflows in one year? And what happens if you get them with different time spaces in between? That's when you need to use XNPV, because this formula allows you to enter as much individual cashflows as you want and with different dates.

WHICH IS THE MAIN BENEFIT OF THIS FORMULA?

You can easily discover the NET PRESENT VALUE, even if you receive the cashflows in different dates of the year

HOW IS THIS FUNCTION STRUCTURED?

The syntax (Structure) of the **XNPV** function is the next one:

=XNPV(rate,values,dates)

WHAT DOES THAT MEAN?

RATE: Is the discount factor (the inflation or the risk-free rate)

VALUES: This is the Range of the values

DATES: This is the Range for the dates of the investment and the cashflows.

Let's try an exercise.

EXERCISE (Open file Chapter5ex2.xlsx)

Similar exercise to the previous one, but this time you will have different cashflow dates.

IRON
MAN

DATES	CASHFLOW
12/01/15	-40000
01/06/16	10000
01/11/16	12000
01/05/17	9000
01/12/18	10000
01/01/20	13000

Step 1: Position yourself in E5 and start writing the formula

=XNPV(

Step 2: Select the discount rate (the inflation cell) E3

$$=XNPV(E3,$$

Step 3: Select the range of EVERY CASHFLOW (including the investment)

$$=XNPV(E3,B4:B9,$$

Step 4: Select the range of EVERY DATE (including the investment), close the parenthesis and press enter.

$$=XNPV(E3,B4:B9,A4:A9)$$

IRON MAN

DATES	CASHFLOW	INFLATION	4%
12/01/15	-40000		
01/06/16	10000	NPV	$8,156.00
01/11/16	12000		
01/05/17	9000		
01/12/18	10000		

01/01/20	13000

Notice that, the NET PRESENT VALUE (with those dates) is greater than the NET PRESENT VALUE of the NPV formula?

Why? Because most of the cashflows were received during the first 2 years and a half, so the inflation didn't affect those cashflows as much as the last 2 cashflows.

TAKING INTO ACCOUNT THE INFLATION AND THE DATE IS EXTREMELY IMPORTANT TO GET AN ACCURATE RESULT OF NET PRESENT VALUE.

Now it is your turn to solve the remaining XNPV of the spreadsheet.

XIRR FUNCTION

WHAT IS THIS FUNCTION FOR?

This function is a used a little bit in conjunction with the XNPV. The IRR stands for "Internal Rate of Return" while the XIRR stands for "Internal Rate of Return with different spaces between cashflows"

The XIRR calculates the Rate of Return that you get with the cashflows from a project. It works almost the same as XNPV but with 2 differences:

- It gives you a %, not a $ number.
- It doesn't take in to account inflation (or risk-free rate) so you need to make sure that the IRR that you get is greater than the inflation.

In simple words, If the XIRR is 4% and the inflation rate is 4% you won't earn money nor lose it. (And you can confirm this calculating the XNPV and you will get a $0.

WHICH IS THE MAIN BENEFIT OF THIS FORMULA?

You can easily discover the RATE of RETURN that you will have with a project (investment) using some cashflows estimates, and you can figure out if the RATE OF RETURN is greater than the inflation.

HOW IS THIS FUNCTION STRUCTURED?

The syntax (Structure) of the **XIRR** function is the next one:

=XIRR(values,dates)

WHAT DOES THAT MEAN?

VALUES: This is the Range of the values

DATES: This is the Range for the dates of the investment and the cashflows.

Let's try an exercise.

EXERCISE (Open file Chapter5ex3.xlsx)

Similar exercise to the previous one, but this time you will have to calculate the INTERNAL RATE OF RETURN for the investments.

IRON

MAN

DATES	CASHFLOW
12/01/15	-40000
01/06/16	10000
01/11/16	12000
01/05/17	9000
01/12/18	10000
01/01/20	13000

Step 1: Position yourself in E5 and start writing the formula

=XIRR(

Step 2: Select the range of EVERY CASHFLOW (including the investment)

=XIRR(B4:B9,

Step 3: Select the range of EVERY DATE (including the investment), close the parenthesis and press enter.

=XIRR(B4:B9,A4:A9)

IRON MAN

DATES	CASHFLOW
12/01/15	-40000
01/06/16	10000
01/11/16	12000
01/05/17	9000
01/12/18	10000
01/01/20	13000

IRR	11%

Notice that the RATE OF RETURN FOR THAT PROJECT IS 11%. That means it is a god project because it is greater than the inflation rate. (Compare that with the XNPV exercise you did before)

TAKING INTO ACCOUNT THE INFLATION AND THE DATE IS EXTREMELY IMPORTANT TO GET AN ACCURATE RESULT OF INTERNAL RATE OF RETURN.

Now it is your turn to solve the remaining XIRR of the spreadsheet.

PMT FUNCTION

WHAT IS THIS FUNCTION FOR?

This function is used for 2 main purposes:

1) To know the monthly payment that you have to make in order to

REPAY a loan you took at a determined interest rate.

2) To know the amount of money you have to invest monthly (at a determined interest rate) in order to get X amount of money.

WHICH IS THE MAIN BENEFIT OF THIS FORMULA?

You can easily discover the amount of money you need to pay or invest.

HOW IS THIS FUNCTION STRUCTURED?

The syntax (Structure) of the **PMT** function is the next one:

=PMT(interest rate,number of periods, loan, goal)

WHAT DOES THAT MEAN?

RATE: Is the interest rate of the investment or the loan

IMPORTANTE NOTE: Normally, those interest rates are Annual BUT they are realized monthly, so you need to divide the Annual interest rate by 12 months. (Example: 12% interest rate divided by 12 months would mean 1% a month. It is the 1% the number that you need, not the 12%)

NUMBER OF PERIODS: Number of months of your loan or investment

LOAN (present value): The total amount of the loan (This is called the principal)

GOAL (future value): The amount of money that you want to get by investing every month

IMPORTANT NOTE: IF YOU ARE

CALCULATING AN INVESTMENT GOAL, YOU NED TO LEAVE EMPTY THE "LOAN ARGUMENT", IF YOU ARE CALCULATING LOAN YOU NEED TO LEAVE EMPTY THE "GOAL ARGUMENT"

Let's try an exercise.

EXERCISE (Open file Chapter5ex4.xlsx)

Our superheroes are tired of fighting and saving the world, so they are planning their retirement. Let's help them to figure out how much money they need to save in order to reach their retirement goals by investing in the S&P500, which has delivered a 9% of average annual.

IRON MAN

RETIREMENT	$5,000,000
ANNUAL RATE	9%

MONTHS	120
SAVINGS NEEDED PER MONTH	

Step 1: Position yourself in B6 and start writing the formula

=PMT(

Step 2: Select the interest rate cell **AND DIVIDE IT BY 12 MONTHS!**

=PMT(B4/12,

Step 3: Select the number of months

=PMT(B4/12,B5,

Step 4: LEAVE THE LOAN ARGUMENT (PRESENT VALUE) EMPY or add a zero.

=PMT(B4/12,B5,0,

Step 5: Then select the desired retirement goal, close the parenthesis and press Enter

=PMT(B4/12,B5,0,B3)

IRON MAN

RETIREMENT	$5,000,000
ANNUAL RATE	9%
MONTHS	120
SAVINGS NEEDED PER MONTH	$25,837.89

Notice that you get a NEGATIVE NUMBER, that means that $25,837 needs to go out of Iron Man's pocket every month, and into his investing account, in order to get $5,000,000 in 10 years!

IMPORTANT NOTE: FOR LOANS IS THE SAME, YOU JUST NEED TO SELECT THE AMOUNT IN THE "LOAN ARGUMENT" AND LEAVE EMPTY (OR WITH A ZERO) THE "GOAL ARGUMENT)

Now solve the other 3 exercises!

IPMT FUNCTION

WHAT IS THIS FUNCTION FOR?

This function is used for 2 main purposes:

1) To discover the monthly interest paid in a loan in a specific month (given a specific interest rate)

2) To discover the monthly interest earned in an investment in a specific month (given a specific interest rate)

WHICH IS THE MAIN BENEFIT OF THIS FORMULA?

You can easily discover the amount interest that you are going to earn or to pay.

HOW IS THIS FUNCTION STRUCTURED?

The syntax (Structure) of the **IPMT** function is the next one:

=IPMT(interest rate,period,number of periods, loan, goal)

WHAT DOES THAT MEAN?

RATE: Is the interest rate of the investment or the loan

IMPORTANTE NOTE: Normally, those interest rates are Annual BUT they are realized monthly, so you need to divide the Annual interest rate by 12 months.

(Example: 12% interest rate divided by 12 months would mean 1% a month. It is the 1% the number that you need, not the 12%)

PERIOD: The month that you want to calculate the interest for.

NUMBER OF PERIODS: Total number of months of your loan or investment

LOAN (present value): The total amount of the loan (This is called the principal)

GOAL (future value): The amount of money that you want to get by investing every month

IMPORTANT NOTE: IF YOU ARE CALCULATING AN INVESTMENT GOAL, YOU NED TO LEAVE EMPTY THE "LOAN ARGUMENT", IF YOU ARE CALCULATING LOAN YOU NEED TO LEAVE EMPTY THE "GOAL ARGUMENT"

Let's try an exercise.

EXERCISE (Open file Chapter5ex5.xlsx)

Now, Aquaman took a loan of $100,000 because he needed a new car, let's try to find out the amount of interest that he will pay in every period and the total amount at the end.

AQUAMAN

LOAN	$100,000
ANNUAL RATE	4%
MONTHS	24

Step 1: Position yourself in F4 and start writing the formula. Notice that we are going to drag the formula so we are going to need some Absolute References.

=IPMT(

Step 2: Select the interest rate cell, **DIVIDE THAT BY 12 MONTHS OF THE YEAR**, and add Absolute references

$$=IPMT(\$B\$4/12,$$

Step 3: Select the period (month) that you want to calculate. In this case you need to select the Month #1 (WITHOUT absolute references because you will need that number to move as you drag the formula)

The cell is E4 and the number inside is 1, so the formula will calculate the interest payment for the month 1. As you drag the formula it will calculate the interest for all the other months.

$$=IPMT(\$B\$4/12,E4,$$

Step 4: Select the number of periods cell and add Absolute references.

=IPMT($B$4/12,E4,$B$5,

Step 5: Select the cell that contains value of the loan and leave empty the "goal argument" because it is not an investment. Finally close the parenthesis, press enter and drag the formula.

=IPMT($B$4/12,E4,$B$5,

MONTH	INTEREST PAID
1	-$333.33
2	-$319.97
3	-$306.56
4	-$293.11

Notice how the interest payments are lower each month (even your monthly payments are flat), that is because at the beginning of a loan, the major part of your payment is for the interest payment.

Great! Let's move to another financial formula!

NPER FUNCTION

WHAT IS THIS FUNCTION FOR?

Its main purpose is to calculate how many months you are going to pay for certain loan at a determined interest rate. Another use for this is to estimate how many months you need to save and invest (at a certain interest rate) to get a certain amount of money.

WHICH IS THE MAIN BENEFIT OF THIS FORMULA?

You can easily discover the number of months you need to pay for a loan or for an investment goal.

HOW IS THIS FUNCTION STRUCTURED?

The syntax (Structure) of the **NPER** function is the next one:

=NPER(interest rate, payment, loan or goal)

WHAT DOES THAT MEAN?

RATE: Is the interest rate of the investment or the loan

IMPORTANTE NOTE: Normally, those interest rates are Annual BUT they are realized monthly, so you need to divide the Annual interest rate by 12 months. (Example: 12% interest rate divided by 12 months would mean 1% a month. It is the 1% the number that you need, not the 12%)

PAYMENT: The monthly payment or savings

LOAN OR GOAL (present value): The

LOAN or the GOAL you want to get.

IMPORTANT NOTE: IF YOU ARE CALCULATING AN INVESTMENT GOAL, YOU NED TO LEAVE EMPTY THE "LOAN ARGUMENT", IF YOU ARE CALCULATING LOAN YOU NEED TO LEAVE EMPTY THE "GOAL ARGUMENT"

Let's try an exercise.

EXERCISE (Open file Chapter5ex6.xlsx)

Now, Goku wants to save $1,000,000 for its retirement. He wants to save $1,500. He found that the S&P500 delivers an average gain of 9% but, because he is conservative, he wants to calculate the NPER with 8% of average gain.

GOKU

GOAL	$1,000,000
ANNUAL RATE	9%
MONTHLY SAVINGS	$ 1,500.00

NUMBER OR MONTHS	

Step 1: Position yourself in B7 and start writing the formula.

$$=NPER($$

Step 2: Select the interest rate cell, **DIVIDE THAT BY 12 MONTHS OF THE YEAR.**

$$=NPR(B4/12,$$

Step 3: Select the monthly savings

$$=IPMT(B4/12,B5$$

Step 4: Select the cell that contains value of the goal. Close the parenthesis and press Enter.

$$=IPMT(B4/12,B5,0,B3)$$

GOKU

GOAL	$1,000,000
ANNUAL RATE	8%
MONTHLY SAVINGS	$ 1,500.00

NUMBER OR MONTHS	-255

Goku needs to make 255 monthly investments of $1,500 to roughly get a $1,000,000 portfolio.

Now it is your turn to solve the exercises for GOHAN, PICOLLO AND TRUNKS!

RECEIVED FUNCTION

WHAT IS THIS FUNCTION FOR?

Its main purpose is to calculate how much money you will get after you invest in Bonds o Bills.

WHICH IS THE MAIN BENEFIT OF THIS FORMULA?

You can easily discover the money yu will get with an investment.

HOW IS THIS FUNCTION STRUCTURED?

The syntax (Structure) of the **RECEIVED** function is the next one:

=RECEIVED(start date, finish date, investment, rate)

WHAT DOES THAT MEAN?

START DATE: The date you invest your money

FINISH DATE: The date the Bond "matures" (The day you get your money plus the interest earned)

INVESTMENT: The amount you invest

RATE: The interest Rate

IMPORTANT NOTE:

BECAUSE IT IS A BOND, YOU WON'T NEED TO DIVIDE THE RATE BY 12. YOU CAN USE THE ANNUAL RATE.

Let's try an exercise.

EXERCISE (Open file Chapter5ex7.xlsx)

Now, Goku wants to invest in Treasury Bonds of USA, as well as Gohan, Picollo and Trunks. They had the option to invest different amounts, with different maturity dates and with different rates.

Let's see how they did.

GOKU

AMOUNT INVESTED	$150,000
ANNUAL RATE	5%
START DATE	01-jul-15
FINISH DATE	01-jul-18
MONEY RECEIVED	

Step 1: Position yourself in B7 and start writing the formula.

=RECEIVED(

Step 2: Select the star date

=RECEIVED(B5,

Step 3: Select the finish date

=RECEIVED(B5,B6

Step 4: Select the cell that contains the investment amount.

=RECEIVED(B5,B6,B3,

Step 5: Select the cell that contains the interest rate, close the parenthesis and press Enter.

=RECEIVED(B5,B6,B3,B4)

GOKU

AMOUNT INVESTED	$150,000
ANNUAL RATE	5%
START DATE	01-jul-15
FINISH DATE	01-jul-18
MONEY RECEIVED	$ 176,470.59

That's the amount of money Goku receives at the end of the investment period.

It is your turn to find the amount for the remaining 3 heroes.

CONGRATULATIONS! YOU DID IT, NOW YOU KNOW HOW TO USE THE MAIN FINANCILA FORMULAS IN EXCEL!

YOU ARE ONE STEP CLOSER OF BECOMING AN EXCEL FORMULAS NINJA!

QUICK CHAPTER SUMMARY:

- Financial formulas help you to take important money decisions at your job and in your personal life

- Remember to take in to account the inflation, as it erodes your purchasing power

- Remember that the compound effect of investing a little bit of money early in your life is more powerful than investing a lot of money later in your life

CHAPTER 6

LOGICAL FORMULAS

This is the chapter where you are going to learn one of the most important logical formulas, the IF formula.

You will also learn other variants of IF that are also considered logical formulas.

Just to be sure we are speaking the same language a logical formula is the one that you use whenever you want to perform a "logical test" and then the formula needs to decide IF it returns option 1 or option 2 based on the previous test it performed.

As always, with the examples is easier to understand.

IF FORMULA

WHAT IS THIS FUNCTION FOR?

Its main purpose is to perform a logical test and after that, return a solution based on the result of the logical test

When you use the IF formula, normally you will use NESTED FORMULAS.

What the hell is a nested formula? Is a formula INSIDE another formula. It is an even more complex way to use formulas but it is worth the time that you invest in learning that.

Basically, the IF formula works like this:

1) IF the logical test is true, it performs a determined calculation (or specific formula) set by you

2) IF the logical test is false, it performs ANOTHER DIFFERENT calculation (or specific formula) set by you.

WHICH IS THE MAIN BENEFIT OF THIS FORMULA?

It is a flexible that will return a result based on a previous logical test.

HOW IS THIS FUNCTION STRUCTURED?

The syntax (Structure) of the **IF** function is the next one:

=IF(logical test, value if true, value if false)

WHAT DOES THAT MEAN?

LOGICAL TEST The test you want to perform in order to know if it is true or false

VALUE IF TRUE: If the logical test is met, then this result will be shown.

VALUE IF FALSE: If the logical test is NOT met, then this result will be shown.

Let's try an exercise.

EXERCISE (Open file Chapter6ex1.xlsx)

Our heroes took a certification exam, so they can continue to work as heroes. If they fail the exam they need to stop working until they pass the exam.

Here have the grades. You need to write "APPROVED" next to the grades if the result is equal or greater than 70, and you need to write "FAILED" is the result is equal or lower than 69.

	GRADES	RESULT
Harry Potter	90	

Captain America	88	
Robin	47	
Captain Marvel	39	
Picollo	92	

Step 1: Position yourself in C3 and start writing the formula.

$$=IF($$

Step 2: Write the logical formula.

How? Well, we want to know if the grade is equal or greater than 70, so we need to use any of these symbols = < > in conjunction with the cells.

First, you need to find out WHERE is the grade. In this case you have it in B3

Then, you need to think about the logical test:

To say equal to 70 we would write: =70

To say greater than 70 we would write: >70

To say equal or greater than 70 we would

write: >=70

To say smaller than 70 we would write: <70

To say equal or smaller than 70 we would write: <=70

So, to say "IF B3 is equal or greater than 70" we would write:

=IF(B3>=70,

Step 3: Set a result if the logical test is TRUE. We want Excel to automatically write APPROVED if the logical test is true.

Then, we need to write it like this *"APPROVED"*

=IF(B3>=70,"APPROVED",

Step 4: Set a result if the logical test is FALSE. We want Excel to automatically write FAILED if the logical test is false.

Then, we need to write it like this *"FAILED"*. Then close the parenthesis and drag the formula.

NOTE: It is not necessary to add Absolute References because you will be testing different grades and you want the formula to move with them.

=IF(B3>=70,"APPROVED","FAILED")

	GRADES	RESULT
Harry Potter	90	APPROVED
Captain America	88	APPROVED
Robin	47	FAILED
Captain Marvel	39	FAILED
Picollo	92	APPROVED

That's it! You automatically wrote all the results you wanted.

Now let's try another exercise but with NESTED FUNCTIONS!

EXERCISE (Open file Chapter6ex2.xlsx)

Our heroes took 4 exams and now we want to analyze the grades. Notice that in cell **A1** you have "average" written. That's is because we want to create a formula that works like this:

- **If A1 has the word "AVERAGE"** then we want the average of the 4 exams
- But **if A1 doesn't have the word "AVERAGE"** then we want the LOWER grade of that hero.

AVERAGE					
	1ST	2ND	3RD	4TH	RESULT
Harry Potter	80	65	89	76	
Captain America	49	85	83	86	
Robin	46	90	88	99	
Captain Marvel	58	81	42	87	

Picollo	98	51	47	60	
Batman	93	76	100	73	

Step 1: Position yourself in F3 and start writing the formula.

$$=IF($$

Step 2: Write the logical formula.

How? Well, we want to know if A1 has the word "AVERAGE" or not. REMEMBER TO ADD ABSOLUTE REFERENCES TO A1 BECAUSE WE DON'T WANT A1 TO MOVE.

So, to say "IF A1 has AVERAGE" we would write:

$$=IF(\$A\$1="AVERAGE",$$

Step 3: Set a result if the logical test is TRUE. We want Excel to automatically calculate the AVERAGE. That's when we use the NESTED FORMULA AVERAGE!

IMPORTANT NOTE:

REMEMBER THAT A NESTED FORMULA IS A FORMULA INSIDE ANOTHER FORMULA.

IN SIMPLE WORDS, THE AVERAGE FORMULA WILL BE PLACED IN THE 2ND ARGUMENT OF THE IF FORMULA.

Then, we need to write an AVERAGE formula (that you already know) in the 2nd Argument of IF.

=IF($A$1="AVERAGE",AVERAGE(B3:
E3),

Notice how you start by writing the name of the AVERAGE formula, open another parenthesis, write the range of cells for the average formula, THEN CLOSE THE PARENTHESIS AGAIN and then write a comma to start the 3rd Argument.

Step 4: Set a result if the logical test is FALSE. Just as we did with the AVERAGE formula, we need to do it with the MINIMUM FORMULA!

=IF($A$1="AVERAGE",AVERAGE(B3: E3),MIN(B3:E3))

Notice how at the end you need to close 2 parenthesis.

Why? Because with the firs one you are closing the MINIMUM FORMULA and with the 2nd one you are closing the complete IF FORMULA.

NOTE: It is not necessary to add Absolute References to average formula nor minimum formula because you will be testing different grades and you want the formula to move with them. Just add absolute references to A1

With AVERAGE in A1

AVERAGE	1ST	2ND	3RD	4TH	RESULT
Harry Potter	80	65	89	76	77.5
Captain America	49	85	83	86	75.75
Robin	46	90	88	99	80.75

Erasing AVERAGE from A1

	1ST	2ND	3RD	4TH	RESULT
Harry Potter	80	65	89	76	65
Captain America	49	85	83	86	49
Robin	46	90	88	99	46

That's it! Let's move forward with the next logical formula!

BY THE WAY, IF FORMULA IS A SUPER USEFUL FORMULA, IT WILL TAKE MUCH MORE THAN THIS TO MASTER IT. SO I WOULD REALLY ENCOURAGE YOU TO GET MY "EXCEL IF FUNCTION CHAMPION" BOOK. IT IS A FULL BOOK GETTING DEEP INTO THIS IF FUNCTION!

"The book was engaging and encouraging by providing many examples and exercises. I will eagerly study the other

books in the series."

IFERROR FORMULA

WHAT IS THIS FUNCTION FOR?

Its main purpose is to catch any errors in another formula (Nested formula). If the formula you want to use is correct, then anything different would happen. But if the formula is incorrect (and has an error) you get to choose the text you want to be displayed.

As an example, you would want Excel to write "Please check your formula", or "Something is wrong with your formula".

WHICH IS THE MAIN BENEFIT OF THIS FORMULA?

It shows a predetermined text if you have an error in your nested formula

The downside to this is that you don't get to see the kind of error that would show up if you hadn't used IFERROR.

HOW IS THIS FUNCTION STRUCTURED?

The syntax (Structure) of the **IFERROR** function is the next one:

=IFERROR(value,value if error)

WHAT DOES THAT MEAN?

VALUE: The cell or the Nested Formula that you want to use

VALUE IF ERROR: The text that you want to show up if you have any errors.

Let's try an exercise.

EXERCISE (Open file Chapter6ex3.xlsx)

Our heroes are working in different

sectors, but the ones that were fired were REMOVED FROM THE DATABASE. So, we are now creating a SEARCH TOOL that displays the name of the sector they are in, for this we are going to use VLOOKUP

If they are not in the data base we would get an error. Instead of an error I want Excel to show "FIRED".

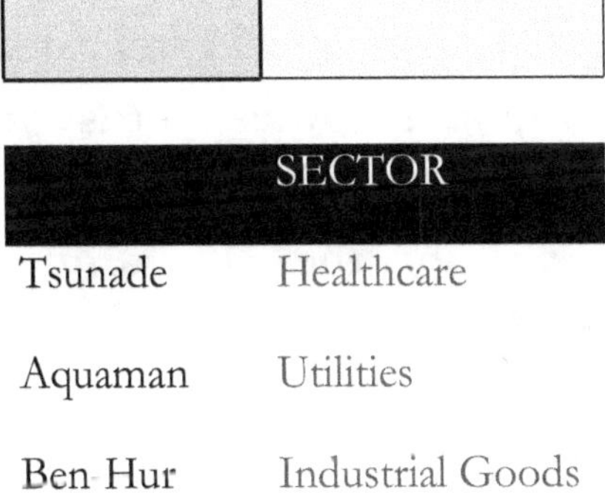

	SECTOR
Tsunade	Healthcare
Aquaman	Utilities
Ben Hur	Industrial Goods
Black Canary	Consumer Goods

Step 1: Position yourself in B1 and start writing the formula.

=IFERROR(

Step 2: Write nested formula VLOOKUP in the 1ˢᵗ argument. If you don't remember how VLOOKUP works you can go back to the SEARCH AND REFERENCE FORMULAS Chapter

=IFERROR(VLOOKUP(A1,A3:C84,2,0),

Notice that VLOOKUP has its own parenthesis and it is all integrated in the first argument. In other words, you need to open and close the VLOOUKUP formula within the 1ˢᵗ argument of IFERROR formula.

Step 3: Write what you what Excel to write if it doesn't find the hero (you would get an error). In this situation you want Excel to write "Fired". Close the parenthesis and press Enter.

=IFERROR(VLOOKUP(A1,A3:C84,2,0)," FIRED")

Hero in the database

ARAGORN	Technology

HERO	SECTOR
Tsunade	Healthcare
Aquaman	Utilities
Ben-Hur	Industrial Goods

Hero that is not in the data base

ANAKIN	FIRED

HERO	SECTOR
Tsunade	Healthcare
Aquaman	Utilities

VLOOKUP without using IFERROR

ANAKIN	#N/A

HERO	SECTOR
Tsunade	Healthcare
Aquaman	Utilities

Now you can use the IFERROR formula to eliminate (hide) the annoying errors. But remember the downside, most of the time you need to deal with those errors and correct them.

COUNTIF FORMULA

WHAT IS THIS FUNCTION FOR?

Its main purpose is to count the cells that match some criteria you establish.

WHICH IS THE MAIN BENEFIT OF THIS FORMULA?

You can easily get the number of items that match your criteria.

HOW IS THIS FUNCTION STRUCTURED?

The syntax (Structure) of the **COUNTIF** function is the next one:

=COUNTIF(Range, Criteria)

WHAT DOES THAT MEAN?

RANGE: The range of cells that you want to count if they met certain criteria.

CRITERIA: The logical test (or text) that you want to be true in order to count that cell.

Let's try an exercise.

EXERCISE (Open file Chapter6ex4.xlsx)

If you remember the first exercise of this chapter, our heroes took a certification exam, so they can continue to work as heroes. They got an "APPROVED" or a "FAILED" according to their grades.

Now, we are going to COUNT how many of them were approved or failed the exam.

APPROVED

FAILED

	GRADES	RESULT
Harry Potter	90	APPROVED
Captain America	88	APPROVED
Robin	47	FAILED

Step 1: Position yourself in B1 and start writing the formula to get the APPROVED ones first.

=COUNTIF(

Step 2: Select the Range of cells you want to count if the criteria is met.

In this situation, you want to count the approved heroes, so you need to select the range that includes both approved and failed.

$$=COUNTIF(C5:C34,$$

Step 3: Set your criteria in the 2nd argument. You can choose between 2 options.

Option 1) Write "APPROVED" in the 2nd argument (because you want to count that.

Option 2) Select Cell A1 because it already contains what you are looking for

Close the parenthesis and press Enter.

$$=IF(B3>=70,"APPROVED",A1)$$

APPROVED	15
FAILED	

	GRADES	RESULT
Harry Potter	90	APPROVED
Captain America	88	APPROVED
Robin	47	FAILED

You easily get the total result of 15 approved heroes. That is how the COUNTIF formula works!

Now it is your turn to get the heroes that failed the exam!

SUMIF FORMULA

WHAT IS THIS FUNCTION FOR?

Its main purpose is to sum the cells that match criteria you stablished.

It is similar to COUNTIF but with one major difference: In SUMIF you have to use 2

Ranges of Cells. One range needs to meet the criteria and the other range is the one that is going to be added together.

WHICH IS THE MAIN BENEFIT OF THIS FORMULA?

You can easily get the total value of items that match your criteria.

HOW IS THIS FUNCTION STRUCTURED?

The syntax (Structure) of the **SUMIF** function is the next one:

=SUMIF(Range, Criteria, Sum Range)

WHAT DOES THAT MEAN?

RANGE: The range of cells that you want to analyze to find out if they meet your criteria

CRITERIA: The logical test (or text) that you want to be true.

SUM RANGE: The range of cells that you want to be added together in case the 1st argument met the criteria.

Let's try an exercise, is going to be easier to explain

EXERCISE (Open file Chapter6ex5.xlsx)

Our heroes have made some money, and they were paid with Stocks, Bonds or Cash.

Our job is to find how much money was paid with stocks, how much with bonds, and how much with cash.

STOCKS	
BONDS	
CASH	

	EARNED RESULT

Harry Potter	$ 762,325	STOCKS
Captain America	$ 245,823	CASH
Robin	$ 712,368	BONDS
Captain Marvel	$ 945,447	STOCKS

Table continues..

Step 1: Position yourself in B1 and start writing the formula to get the STOCKS ones first

=SUMIF(

Step 2: Select the Range of cells that contains the criteria. (The range with STOCKS, CASH and BONDS)

=SUMIF(C6:C35,

Why? Because that range will tell Excel if the criteria is met or not.

Step 3: Set your criteria in the 2nd argument. You can choose between 2 options.

Option 1) Write "STOCKS" in the 2nd argument

Option 2) Select Cell A1 because it already contains what you are looking for

$$=SUMIF(C6:C35,A1,$$

Step 4: Select the SUM RANGE. This range contains the cells with the money earned by the heroes. **You need this range because Excel will sum that money if it is in the same ROW of that with "STOCKS" label.**

$$=SUMIF(C6:C35,A1,B6:B36)$$

Close the parenthesis and press enter.

STOCKS	$ 3,672,476
BONDS	
CASH	

	EARNED	RESULT
Harry Potter	$ 762,325	STOCKS
Captain America	$ 245,823	CASH
Robin	$ 712,368	BONDS
Captain Marvel	$ 945,447	STOCKS

What exactly happened?

1) Excel searched for the word "STOCKS" in range **C6:C35**
2) If any ROW had that word, then Excel added the money that is in Column B and in that same ROW
3) At the end, you get the sum of all money paid in STOCKS.

Now it is your turn to calculate the money earned in BONDS and in CASH! Follow the same instructions and do it.

CONGRATULATIONS! **YOU**

ALREADY KNOW HOW TO USE THE MOST IMPORTANT LOGICAL FORMULAS IN EXCEL!

IT IS TIME TO GO TO THE LAST SET OF FORMULAS.

QUICK CHAPTER SUMMARY:

- Logical formulas save a lot of time when used correctly
- Nested Functions are an essential part when using the IF Formula
- COUNT IF and SUMIF are very similar, but SUMIF is a little more complex

CHAPTER 7

TEXT FORMULAS

CONGRATULATIONS for making it this far. The most complex formulas were described in the previous chapters.

This chapter is the easier one, and it is all about formatting text. You won't find that many situations where you need to use all of these formulas, but it is better to be prepared, because they are so easy to learn.

LEFT, AND RIGHT FORMULAS

WHAT ARE THESE FUNCTIONS

FOR?

Their main purpose is to extract X number of characters from a given text or word.

The LEFT formula starts from the left

The RIGHT formula starts from the right.

WHICH IS THE MAIN BENEFIT OF THESE FORMULAS?

You can easily extract the characters you want if you need to.

HOW IS THIS FUNCTION STRUCTURED?

The syntax (Structure) of the **LEFT and RIGHT** functions is the next one:

=LEFT(text, number of characters to extract)

=RIGHT(text, number of characters to extract)

WHAT DOES THAT MEAN?

TEXT: The text or the cell where you have the text.

NUMBER OF CHARACTERS: How many characters do you want to extract?

Let's try an exercise

EXERCISE (Open file Chapter7ex1.xlsx)

Let's say you want to extract the first 2 letters of the Hero's name. Then you would need to use the LEFT formula.

HERO	SECTOR
Harry Potter	Healthcare

Captain America	Utilities
Robin	Industrial Goods
Captain Marvel	Consumer Goods
Picollo	Financial

Step 1: Position yourself in E3 and start writing the formula

$$=LEFT($$

Step 2: Select the Cell with the first hero name

$$=LEFT(A3$$

Step 3: Write the number of characters you want to extract. In this case you write 2. Close the parenthesis and press Enter!

$$=LEFT(A3,2)$$

HERO 2 LEFT	HERO 2 RIGHT
Ha	

That's it. It was incredibly easy.

Now imagine that you want the LAST 2 characters of the name. Then you would need to use the RIGH formula. (It works exactly the same as LEFT).

$$=RIGHT(A3,2)$$

HERO 2 LEFT	HERO 2 RIGHT
Ha	er
Ca	ca
Ro	in

If you drag the formula, you'll get them all.

On your own, complete the whole excrcise. It has no difficulty.

MID FORMULA

WHAT IS THIS FUNCTION FOR?

Its main purpose is to extract X number of characters from a given text or word.

You can start extracting characters from the middle of the text.

WHICH IS THE MAIN BENEFIT OF THIS FORMULA?

You can easily extract the characters you want if you need to.

HOW IS THIS FUNCTION STRUCTURED?

The syntax (Structure) of the **MID** function is the next one:

=MID(text, start, number of characters)

WHAT DOES THAT MEAN?

TEXT: The text or the cell where you have the text.

START: The position where you want to start. If you write 2, MID will start extracting from the 2nd character of the text.

NUMBER OF CHARACTERS: How many characters do you want to extract?

Let's try an exercise

EXERCISE (Open file Chapter7ex2.xlsx)

Similar exercise to the previous one. Let's extract some characters!

Start in 2

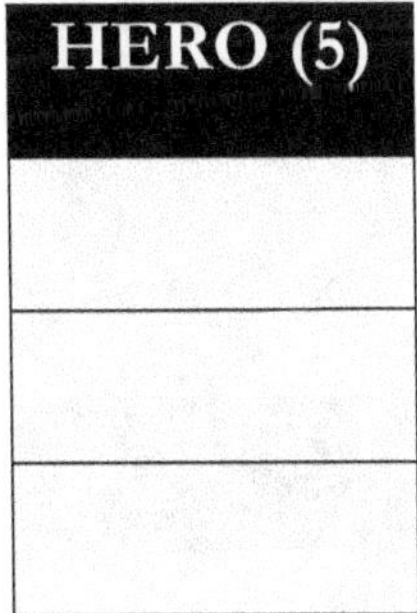

We need to start in the 2nd character and

extract 5 characters.

Step 1: Position yourself in E3 and start writing the formula

$$=MID($$

Step 2: Select the Cell with the first hero name

$$=MID(A3$$

Step 3: Write the position there you want to start extracting.

$$=MID(A3,2,$$

Step 4: Write the number of characters you want to extract. In this case you write 5. Close the parenthesis and press Enter.

$$=MID(A3,2,5)$$

Start in 2

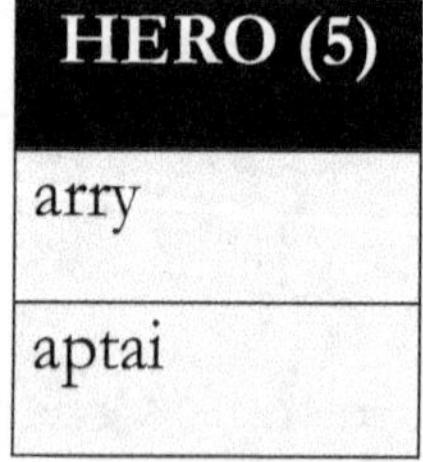

HERO (5)
arry
aptai

> obin

Notice that in the first one (**H*arry*** Potter) the SPACE was counted as one character. That is how the formula works

Now complete the exercise by yourself.

TRIM FORMULA

WHAT IS THIS FUNCTION FOR?

Its main purpose is to delete unnecessary spaces between words.

Sometimes, when you get a spreadshect, you get this king of errors with unnecessary extra spaces between words.

WHICH IS THE MAIN BENEFIT OF THIS FORMULA?

You can easily delete spaces between

text.

HOW IS THIS FUNCTION STRUCTURED?

The syntax (Structure) of the **TRIM** function is the next one:

$$=TRIM(text)$$

WHAT DOES THAT MEAN?

TEXT: The text or the cell where you want to delete spaces.

EXERCISE (Open file Chapter7ex3.xlsx)

You have a lot of spaces between text. Without TRIM, you would need to erase them manually. But you can use TRIM formula to do it fast.

HERO

Harry   Potter   is   famous   in England
Captain   America   and   Iron Man   are not friends anymore
Robin   hates   Batman
Captain   Marvel   is   overpowered

Step 1: Position yourself in C3 and start writing the formula

=TRIM(

Step 2: Select the Cell where you want to erase spaces, close the parenthesis and drag the formula

=TRIM(A3)

TRIM
Harry Potter is famous in England
Captain America and Iron Man are not friends anymore
Robin hates Batman
Captain Marvel is overpowered

That's it. This is the easiest formula in the entire book!

UPPER, LOWER AND PROPER FORMULAS

WHAT ARE THESE FUNCTIONS FOR?

Their main purpose is to transform the text in to UPPER CASE letters, LOWER CASE letters and PROPER NAME format.

WHICH ARE THE MAIN BENEFIT OF THESE FORMULAS?

You can easily change the format to UPPER CASE, LOWER CASE or PROPER NAME

HOW ARE THESE FUNCTIONS STRUCTURED?

The syntax (Structure) of is the next one:

=UPPER(text)

=LOWER(text)

=PROPER(text)

WHAT DOES THAT MEAN?

TEXT: The text you want to transform.

EXERCISE (Open file Chapter7ex3.xlsx)

Let's transform the text!

HERO	UPPER	LOWER	PROPER
Harry potter			

Captain america			
Robin			
Captain marvel			

Step 1: Position yourself in C3 and start writing the formula

=UPPER(

Step 2: Select the Cell with the name of the hero. Close the parenthesis and drag the formula

=UPPER(A3)

UPPER
HARRY POTTER
CAPTAIN AMERICA
ROBIN
CAPTAIN MARVEL
PICOLLO

Fast and easy! Now do the same with the LOWER formula and with the PROPER formula

UPPER	LOWER	PROPER
HARRY POTTER	harry potter	Harry Potter
CAPTAIN AMERICA	captain america	Captain America
ROBIN	robin	Robin
CAPTAIN MARVEL	captain marvel	Captain Marvel

That's it! Now you can transform text easily!

TEXTJOIN FORMULA

WHAT IS THIS FUNCTION FOR?

Its main purpose is to join the text of multiple cells into one cell

WHICH IS THE MAIN BENEFIT OF THIS FORMULA?

The main advantage here is that you can omit empty cells and you can set a default symbol to separate each cell (although all of them will be in one cell) like a comma.

HOW IS THIS FUNCTION STRUCTURED?

The syntax (Structure) of the **TEXTJOIN** function is the next one:

=TEXTJOIN(delimiter,ignore empty, text cells)

WHAT DOES THAT MEAN?

DELIMITER: The symbol you want to use to separate the text

IGNORE EMPTY: We need to use TRUE if we want to ignore empty cells and FALSE if we don't. The most common is to ignore them.

TEXT CELLS: You can use the range of cells that you are going to join.

EXERCISE (Open file Chapter7ex4.xlsx)

Now, we have the information of our heroes and we need to join all of that in one cell. Notice that some information is missing, but we need to join what we have.

HERO	CITY	CELL PHONE
Optimus Prime	Arlington	(990) 935-8105
Naruto Uzumaki		(962) 210-3462
Batgirl	Oakland	

Step 1: Position yourself in D3 and start writing the formula

=TEXTJOIN(

Step 2: Write the delimiter (the symbol with which you want to separate the text). In this situation we want to use a comma, and we need to do it with this: ", "

Why? Because we need the " " to show excel that we want to use a comma and a space as a TEXT! And after that you need to use another comma that ends the first argument.

$$=TEXTJOIN(", ",$$

Step 3: Write TRUE, because you want to IGNORE the empty cells.

$$=TEXTJOIN(", ",TRUE,$$

Step 4: Select the range of cells you want to join. Then close the parenthesis and press Enter. Then drag the formula down.

$$=TEXTJOIN(", ",TRUE,A3:C3)$$

TEXTJOIN
Optimus Prime, Arlington, (990) 935-8105
Naruto Uzumaki, (962) 210-3462
Batgirl, Oakland

Notice how easy you have put together all the cells. And it doesn't matter if one cell is empty, the formula will omit that.

QUICK CHAPTER SUMMARY:

- TEXT formatting functions are not widely used, but they are so easy to learn that it's better to learn to use them

CHAPTER 8

QUICK FINAL TIPS

CONGRATULATIONS!! You finished the exercises and now you are an EXCEL FORMULAS NINJA! It was a great journey.

This book wouldn't be complete without a series of final recommendations that can help you even more

Here (in this short chapter) I can't teach you everything I'm going to recommend because they are extensive topics that would not fit in a few pages, it is also information that I teach deeply in other Excel books.

However, I want to make the following recommendations you with the hope that you recognize the main tools that you must learn to be an Excel Champion.

WHY DO YOU NEED TO LEARN KEYBOARD PIVOT TABLES?

Pivot Tables are the go-to tools for advanced data analysis! Whenever you are immersed in a gigantic amount of data and you need to take decisions based on that data, Pivot Tables are the way to go!

You can summarize thousands of rows and columns (literally thousands) in just a few seconds. You also can shape your summary to every imaginable way, in order to get relevant insight about your data.

Base your decisions in facts, not opinions! Buy your Pivot Tables Champion copy here!

"THIS BOOK IS SO GREAT! NOW I CAN ANALYZE GIANT DATABASES WITHIN SECONDS!" - Sales Coordinator of a Wholesale Company.

WHY DO YOU NEED TO LEARN KEYBOARD SHORTCUTS?

First of all I want to recommend that you learn Excel keyboard shortcuts. Keyboard shortcuts are the easiest and fastest way to increase your productivity in Excel. You can easily cut your work time in half.

The reality is that there are more than 100 keyboard shortcuts. My recommendation is that you learn the 10 or 20 main ones. Which are the main ones? The ones you use the most depending the kind of work you have to do in Excel.

Some of those that everybody should use are:

Ctrl + C to copy a cell (with format too)

Ctrl + V to paste the cell that you copied

Ctrl + X to cut the cell (instead of copying it, you remove it from its cell to paste it in another cell)

Ctrl + to insert a column or row (selecting the column or row previously)

Ctrl – to delete a column or row (selecting the column or row previously)

Surely with these shortcuts you can move a little faster. But there are more that are quite useful.

WHY DO YOU NEED TO LEARN CONDITIONAL FORMATTING?

You will agree that the human eye identifies faster the colors and shapes than numbers. For the same reason, traffic lights have colors instead of numbers or words.

The conditional formatting in Excel is used to add colors or shapes when certain conditions are met, making the data user-friendly and giving the opportunity to recognize patterns within the data.

Imagine for a moment that you have a table with 100 data and you need to find the values that are closest to the average.

Option 1: The first option is to use the AVERAGE function and then manually search for those values within the table.

Option 2: The fastest and easiest option is to use Conditional Format so that Excel automatically colors the data that is closest to the average, and that's it, you'll have the data you need highlighted in the color you want in a few seconds, it doesn't matter if your table has 100, 1000 or 10000 numbers.

If you would like to search for the 10 highest values within a table, you can do so. If you would like to focus only on data that is less than the average, you can color them automatically. If you want to identify the data that are between 2 values, you can do it in less than 30 seconds.

That is why I recommend conditional formatting. Becoming a Conditional Formatting Champion will allow you to find the most relevant information.

Get your copy of Conditional Formatting Champion here!

"THIS GREAT AND EASY TO UNDERSTAND BOOK TEACHES A VERY USEFUL WAY TO ANALYZE DATA" - *Accounting Manager of a Sportswear Company*

WHY DO YOU NEED TO LEARN TO USE CHARTS?

Charts are, by excellence, the way to communicate quantitative information in the business world, in non-profit organizations, in schools, in governmental organizations, in health areas, in sports, etc.

It's very simple, if you want to effectively communicate your numerical data, you need to master the Excel Charts. That includes the use of tables and the correct positioning of them, the selection of the data that you need, the Chart Type selection and the modification of the parameters of the chart.

Additionally it becomes necessary that you learn to discover what a chart wants to "tell you". Correctly analyzing the data in a chart usually leads to better decisions.

If you want to make better decisions in your job or company, it is very likely that becoming an Excel Charts and Graphs Champion will benefit you.

I WOULD LOVE TO READ YOUR COMMENTS

Before you go, I would like to tell you Thank You for buying my book. It is my wish that the information you obtained in **EXCEL FORMULAS NINJA** helps you in your job or business, and that you can have greater productivity and more free time to use it in the activities that you like the most.

I realize that you could have chosen among several other Excel books but you chose **EXCEL FORMULAS NINJA** and you invested your time and effort. I am honored to have the opportunity to help you.

I'd like to ask you a small favor. **Could you take a minute or two and leave a Review of EXCEL FORMULAS NINJA on Amazon?**

This feedback will be very appreciated and will help me continue to write more courses that help you and a lot more people.

Share your comments with me and other readers

ABOUT THE AUTHOR

Henry E. Mejia is passionate about progress and goal achieving, he also loves to run and exercise. He works in the insurance industry and likes to invest in the stock market. While doing that, he devotes some time to create Excel written courses like this one, in order to help people to achieve their professional goals.

Henry also realized that the vast majority of people use a lot of their work time in front of the computer. That time could be used in more productive or more enjoyable activities, only if people knew how to use Excel a little better.

The goal of Henry's books is to open the door for workers and business owners to use Excel more efficiently, so they can have more and better growth opportunities, progress and free time.